1976

ook may be kept

FOURTEEN DAYS

or each day

BISMARCK AND STATE SOCIALISM

BISMARCK AND STATE SOCIALISM

*AN EXPOSITION OF THE SOCIAL AND
ECONOMIC LEGISLATION OF
GERMANY SINCE* 1870

BY

WILLIAM HARBUTT DAWSON

NEW YORK

Howard Fertig

1973

First published in 1890
Howard Fertig, Inc. Edition 1973
Published by arrangement with
George Allen & Unwin Ltd.
All rights reserved.

Library of Congress Cataloging in Publication Data
Dawson, William Harbutt, 1860-1948.
    Bismarck and state socialism.
    Reprint of the 1890 ed. published by Swan
Sonnenschein, London.
    Includes bibliographical references.
    1. Socialism in Germany. 2. Bismarck, Otto
Fürst von, 1815-1898.   3.   Germany—Economic policy.
I.   Title.
HX273.D2   1973   335.5′0943   70-80539

"I need very little recognition, and am tolerably unsusceptible against criticism."—*June* 2, 1865.

"At any rate it must be allowed that I have always expressed my convictions decidedly, clearly, and openly."—*December* 17, 1873.

"I am a statesman who subordinates himself to the needs and requirements of the State in the interest of the peace and prosperity of my Fatherland."—*December* 17, 1873.

"I have always endeavoured to learn new things, and when I have as a consequence had to correct an earlier opinion, I have done it at once, and I am proud to have done so, for I ever place my country before my person."—*March* 28, 1874.

"I aim at definite, positive, practical ends."—*October* 9, 1878.

"For my part I shall certainly follow to the end the way which I believe to be the best in my country's interest ; whether my reward be hatred or love, is all the same to me."—*July* 9, 1879.

"I do my duty and await the result."—*April* 2, 1881.

—From Prince Bismarck's Speeches.

CONTENTS.

CHAPTER IX.

CHAPTER X.

CHAPTER XI.

APPENDIX.

PREFACE.

THIS volume is intended to be a sequel to a work which
I completed two years ago, and which appeared with the
title "German Socialism and Ferdinand Lassalle: a
Biographical History of German Socialistic Movements
during this Century." In that work—the marked friendli-
ness of whose reception, both in England and Germany,
was the more encouraging because not looked for—an
endeavour was made to show how the seed of a politico-
economical Socialism had found its way to German soil,
how it had germinated, how grown from plant to tree,
and finally to describe the fruit which the tree had borne
and is still bearing.

In the main the survey extended to Social-Democratic
movements, and it did not seem pertinent to the scheme
originally contemplated to devote more than passing
reference to developments like State Socialism, Socialism
of the Chair, and Christian Socialism. From the first,
however, it was my intention to discuss State Socialism
in a second volume, which should be the complement of
its predecessor. A number of causes have prevented the
speedier fulfilment of that intention, yet the delay has
been advantageous rather than the reverse. Since the

work on "German Socialism and Ferdinand Lassalle"
was finished, great political changes have taken place in
Germany. Two Emperors have died, and after passing
through a period of suspense and anxiety unexampled
in its history, the new Empire is to-day ruled by a young
monarch who has been called suddenly and without fore-
warning to undertake duties among the highest and most
responsible that can fall to man—duties, I will venture to
add, to the discharge of which he has already brought
a sagacity, a far-sightedness, and an earnestness that
augur well for the future of his government and his
country.

Moreover, there has recently taken place an event which
will mark the beginning of a new era in German politics.
After faithfully serving his sovereign and nation for
nearly thirty years as First Minister of the Crown in
Prussia, and for twenty as Chancellor of the German
Empire, and after playing a conspicuous part in European
history for at least four decades, Prince Bismarck has at
last sought the retirement and rest which weight of years
and physical weakness long ago entitled him to enjoy.
His masterly guidance of foreign affairs and his epoch-
making development of domestic policy become, therefore,
completed chapters in German political history. We are
now able to view the Chancellor's structure of social and
economic reform, as built up since the re-establishment
of the Empire, while it still exhibits uniform workman-
ship—while it is still the achievement of one brain and
one hand. A few years hence and German State Social-

ism can no longer be exactly the State Socialism of Prince Bismarck. The building he has raised must, in the nature of things, undergo change, both by modification and addition. The following pages describe the ideal after which Bismarck strove, but which he cannot be said yet to have realised. The Chancellor's withdrawal from official life leaves us a scheme of social reform incomplete, it is true, if compared with his ultimate purposes, yet uniform and cognate, like a painting perfect in idea, yet unfinished, needing finer touches here and greater detail there. Bismarck's part in re-shaping the domestic policy of his country may now be regarded as belonging to the past, and it is no longer premature to estimate his position as a social reformer.

Conversing several years ago with Professor Adolph Wagner, who has long and worthily filled a chair of political economy at the Berlin University, and who is generally, and with right, regarded as the foremost scientific exponent of State Socialism in Germany, a word of mine drew from him the remark that State Socialism would be better termed a *Richtung* than a *Schule*—a *direction* than a *school*. This designation involves two distinct ideas. Not only does State Socialism represent a particular development of economic thought, but it describes the entire tenor of recent social and economic legislation in Germany. Bearing this fact in mind, I have approached the subject from both the theoretical and the practical standpoint; and in characterising the laws which belong to what may be called the Bismarck era of social reform, I have always kept antecedent measures in view. It is a great mistake to conclude that Prince Bismarck's State Socialistic projects left his head fully matured as armed Minerva left the head of Jupiter. Without exception they were the result of organic development. What the German Chancellor did was to carry social and economic policy forward on existing lines, or to revert to principles temporarily forsaken. As to the success and permanent value of most of his measures we can as yet do little more than speculate, for sufficient time has not elapsed to allow of accurate judgment. It is significant, however, that laws and institutions which at their inception excited widespread apprehension and opposition have lived down ill-repute, and now receive approbation where formerly they met with hostility. Embarking on a policy of State Socialism in the hope of grappling with Social Democracy, Prince Bismarck was assured both by friends and enemies that he was seeking to cast out a devil with the prince of the devils. Yet in spite of opposition on the one hand, and discouragement on the other, he has, with unflinching confidence and remarkable tenacity of purpose, persisted in the course to which he committed himself and his country more than a decade ago, and the best proof of his statesmanlike foresight and wisdom is to be found in the endorsement of his policy by three successive Emperors and by an ever-growing majority of his countrymen.

Since the appearance of the work whose sequel is the present volume, I have been able to investigate more carefully than had up to that time been possible the State Socialistic measures passed under the new Empire—conducting my inquiries as before in Germany—and I would like to repeat with emphasis the estimate of Prince Bismarck and his social reforms to which I have elsewhere given expression.

" While we must defer judgment upon his policy, we may at once admit that he is the first German statesman who has really tried during the last sixty or seventy years to improve the lot of the labouring population. More than that, he is the first European statesman who has dared to take the social problem in hand with the determination, not indeed to solve it—for that is a task which he himself has admitted will require generations—but to pave the way for solution. . . . There can be little doubt that Prince Bismarck has discovered where the roots of the social evil lie. He has declared, in words that burn, that it is the duty of the State to give heed, above all, to the welfare of its weaker members ; he has vowed that no opposition and no obloquy shall ever deter him from giving practical proof of that conviction ; and he has already advanced a good step on the way of State Socialism, in which he and thousands of thinking men with him alone see hope for the future of society and civilisation, whether in Germany or elsewhere. . . . Whatever opinion we may after full consideration form of the Chancellor's internal policy, we must allow to the man himself the virtue of sincerity, a virtue not always characteristic in these days of the public acts of

statesmen. Further, philanthropy and charity demand
that we shall wish him success in the great undertaking
upon which he has embarked, an undertaking whose
objects are none less than the removal of the wrongs of
a vast and ever-increasing class, and the restoration of
peace to a great country."

W. H. D.

NOTE.—In regard to the authorities for this work, as it deals
largely with legislation, I have relied in the main upon Parliamentary
Reports and Papers, which I have consulted at first hand. I may,
however, say with accuracy that no German work, large or small,
bearing upon the questions considered has been overlooked, though
not many references are given in the following pages. Here I
desire to acknowledge with gratitude the uniform and marked
courtesy shown by the authorities of the Royal Library in Berlin
during an extended period of research.

BISMARCK AND STATE SOCIALISM

CHAPTER I.

THEORY OF STATE SOCIALISM.

In considering the place which State Socialism should occupy in a genealogy of economic systems, we shall be greatly aided if we remember that it is a perfectly organic development. It does not begin with a *tabula rasa*, or build up its structure of theory upon foundations prepared by a Cartesian negation of all existing beliefs. On the contrary, it is a product and a consequence of the past. The State Socialistic school occupies an essentially eclectic position. Adopting the leading principle underlying the historical method,—which may be regarded as having heralded this latest direction,—it enforces the relativity of economic doctrines, and rejecting no economic institution as intrinsically bad, and accepting none as intrinsically good, it seeks to gain recognition, both theoretically and practically, for those principles which investigation, analogy, and experience commend as expedient for the present time.

With the historical school State Socialists hold that in dealing with political economy we are not dealing with an exact science. Phrases such as "orthodox economy," "conventional economy," and the like, have no objective meaning, but represent only the economic conceptions of those who use them. There is no ultimate court of appeal before which economic doctrines can be arraigned in order to receive the verdict, "This is orthodox," or "This is heterodox."

In economics as a science we have to do less with absolute truth than with relative validity. One of the leading scientific exponents of State Socialism in Germany, who is also one of the foremost of that country's living economists, Gustav Schmoller[1]— professor of political economy at the University of Berlin— reminds us that "the smaller part of the teachings of political economy consists of scientifically established propositions ; the larger part of dogmas which are believed by some and rejected by others, according to their party sympathies.   All so-called political, moral, economical, and social principles are not so much the results of exact science as the deduced isolated doctrines of the systems and contemplations of the world held by schools and parties : as the principles of freedom, authority, and justice, the principle of free competition, that of division of labour, that of labour-union ; thus the doctrines of Adam Smith are the economic party-doctrines of Individualism and Liberalism."   There are, however, two economic and philosophical estimates of society with which State Socialism may be brought into broad contrast. While Individualism restricts the functions of the State as much as possible, Socialism enlarges them; the Individualist would do everything without the State, the Socialist would do everything with it.   State Socialism is the mean between these directions of thought ; in it the two extremes meet.   It seeks to abstract from Individualism so much as is necessary to the cultivation of individuality, and from Socialism so much as is required in order to give to manhood a fair chance of development.

The great disagreement between Socialism and State Socialism is that the former would entirely subvert the State, while the latter accepts its political form as it is.   Socialism would abolish the existing political order altogether, while State Socialism would use the State for the accomplishment of great economic and social purposes, especially restoring to it the function, which Frederick the Great held to be the principal business of the State, of "hold-

---

[1] Schmoller's views on this subject are set forth at length in his work "Über einige Grundfragen des Rechts und der Volkswirthschaft," a reply to Heinrich von Treitschke's attack on "The Well-wishers of Socialism" (Jena, 1875).

ing the balance" (*tenir la balance*) between classes and parties. Thus we find Schmoller extolling the polity dominant in Germany, and expressing the conviction that "a firm monarchy is a great blessing for a country when it is bound up with traditions like those of the Prussian monarchy, which recognises its duties."

Again, as to Individualism, State Socialists would restrict the play of self-interest and egoism in the economic domain. Adopting the principle of the greatest happiness of the greatest number, they place the welfare of the community before that of the individual; the ideal should be *extensive* rather than *intensive* material prosperity. Importance is inevitably attached to ethics as a factor in economic dealings. What is morally wrong and culpable should not be regarded as economically right and justifiable.

To use the words of Adolph Wagner, the foremost scientific representative of State Socialism in Germany, "The relation of man to man should again be asserted in the economic relationships between various persons."[1] Or, quoting from an academic colleague of that writer, Schmoller, State Socialism purposes "the re-establishment of a friendly relationship between social classes, the removal or modification of injustice, a nearer approach to the principle of distributive justice, with the introduction of a social legislation which promotes progress and guarantees the moral and material elevation of the lower and middle classes."[2]

It is important to bear in mind that though the term State Socialism is frequently, and not unnaturally, associated with the industrial legislation passed by Prince Bismarck during the past ten years, as though it signified nothing else, this economic movement extends to many directions. Everywhere the social idea is conspicuous. According to Wagner, indeed, we have now entered the "social period," which is "characterised by new economic ideas, new political views, and a new direction in practical life." The claims of society as opposed, or as superior, to those of the individual, should therefore receive prior consideration. Economic institutions are to be judged from the standpoint of the public weal. The standard is not, "What will

---

[1] "Rede über die sociale Frage," p. 8.
[2] "Uber einige Grundfragen," p. 92.

be good for the individual citizen?" but "What will most benefit the whole community?" By their social value, their capacity for promoting social welfare, must the plexus of institutions, organisations, and arrangements, in and by means of which the economic life of the nation is carried on, be tried. Extended State activity in the economic domain is a necessary consequence of this estimate of society. Social interests can only be properly safeguarded when the State directly concerns itself with them. The aim must, therefore, be to widen the economic jurisdiction of the State. In Wagner's words, the task of the time is to make "national economy" (*Volkswirthschaft*) rather "State economy" (*Staatswirthschaft*). The non-intervention principle must be abandoned, since it has only led to greater and ever greater class and personal inequalities, and therefore to growing social disorganisation and discontent. The State Socialists do not, like the Socialists, propose to reduce mankind to a dead level of monotonous uniformity. They recognise the existence of individual differences, yet say that many of these are quite as much the result of civilisation—the result of social and economic institutions—as they are natural. Inequalities not due to the natural peculiarities of the individual should be checked, discouraged, and counteracted. "The weak in the economic struggle," to quote Prince Bismarck's phrase, are entitled to help and protection according to their necessities. Not the strong and efficient but the feeble and defective parts of the social machinery need the special care of the State. Apart, however, from the strictly ethical characteristics of State Socialism, there is the purely economic side. The State may adopt measures, legislative and otherwise, directly intended to further the nation's material interests, as, for instance, in the domain of home or foreign trade, or it may itself take part in the processes of production and distribution. No department of economic activity should on principle be closed to the State ; whether it should or not participate, side by side with private enterprise, is a matter of expediency and public interest. Where the State cannot with advantage undertake economic functions, they may be suited to public bodies, the principle of collectivism being still asserted.

We should not expect the advocates of so liberal an economy

as State Socialism to be unanimous as to the application of the
principles common to all of them. A school which comprises
men of such different minds as Wagner, Schmoller, Albert
Schäffle, Gustav Schönberg, and Held, could not by any possibility preserve agreement in matters of detail. Moreover, the
cloak of State Socialism is thrown over the tatters of many
theories and proposals, wild or at least unpractical, for which
the scientific representatives of the system should not be made
responsible. It is evident that the principles of State intervention
in economic affairs and State care and protection for the poorer
classes being posited, it is difficult to say how far these principles
should be carried. The State Socialists say that this must be
determined by expediency, and by circumstances of time and
place. Yet even here we stand on very insecure ground, and
it must always be more or less a matter of subjective judgment
beyond what limits the State may not with advantage and pro-
priety go. Instead, therefore, of comparing the positions of the
leading representatives of this school of political economists in
Germany, it will be more useful to glance at the main doctrines
advanced by the man who has done more than any one else
to give to State Socialism at once scientific form and scientific
foundation, Adolph Wagner.[1]

Wagner, it should be premised, is prepared to extend the
province of government beyond the limits set by most economists
of his direction.[2] He lays especial emphasis upon the untena-
bility of the idea of finality in economic institutions. In esti-
mating the value of economic principles, it seldom becomes a
question of " either, or ; " it is rather a matter of " more or less."
The bounds of the State's functions have not, like the earth's
foundations, been fixed from of old, that they should not be
removed. The jurisdiction of government is a matter not of

---

[1] Wagner's views are fully set forth in his " Lehrbuch der politischen
Ökonomie " and in his " Finanzwissenschaft " (vol. ii.), where he deals with
the theory of taxation ; but concise and popular summaries of his State
Socialistic theories and proposals are contained in his " Rede über die sociale
Frage," published in 1872, and in articles in the *Tübinger Zeitschrift* for 1887.

[2] See Wagner's " Grundlegung," chap. iv., part 1, sec. 163, where he lays
down seven propositions regarding the functions of the State.

principle but of expediency. Wagner entirely rejects Kant's State, with its narrow functions, but he will not accept the eudemonistic ideal of Wolf as applicable to the present. He opposes the State's passivity in social affairs on the one hand, and he deprecates extreme intervention on the other. He takes his stand upon "the ground of the existing" (*der Boden der Wirklichkeit*), acknowledging the social and economic system and the civil law which are in vogue, with the reservation that they must undergo further organic development. He advocates a reform which, to use his own words, "is neither subversion, nor stagnation, nor retrogression." With Wagner the social question in reality resolves itself into the amelioration of the working classes, and it is essentially on their behalf that he calls for greater State activity in the domain of economics. Self-help is laudable and desirable, and he would encourage it in every way. He grants the right of coalition, and expects much from the development in Germany of trades-unionism and co-operation. Organisation and combination may be rough and ready weapons wherewith to carry on struggles between capital and labour, but as the capitalists swear by the doctrine of free competition, it is but logical to allow to the working classes the arbitrament of coalition, and, if necessary, of the strike. He holds that the State has no right, and no interest, to discourage labour combinations which restrict themselves to economic purposes ; all it can fairly do is to prevent and punish excess, violence, and menace. But self-help, though admirable so far as it goes, is not enough. Unaided the working classes will never achieve their emancipation from capitalistic fetters. The assistance of the State is necessary, and that assistance should be given in no stinted measure. Incidentally, it may be noted that Wagner does not allow that free competition is an unmixed blessing. Its advantages are great, but they have in the past been exaggerated, and they are also accompanied by many serious disadvantages. He would not dream of going back to the guild system, thus renouncing some of the best results of the modern system of production, but he is prepared to consider whether a certain restriction of personal freedom might not be beneficial in such matters as migration and settlement (in order to prevent over-population in towns, to the disadvantage of the country), marriage (so as to check premature and improvident unions), and even handicraft (in the interest of more skilful and con scientious production).

The great thought which underlies Wagner's proposals of economic and social reform is the "ethical factor" which, in his opinion, should be considered in the settlement of economic problems. He laments and condemns the existing "moral indifferentism in the domain of economic dealings." It is not enough to talk of buying and selling labour, and to give and receive money for labour as its price ; we must remember that the relation of employer and employed, of producer and consumer, is that of man to man. To him the idea of "regarding labour-power as a commodity and wages as its price is not only unchristian, but is inhuman in the worst sense of the word." [1] He says plainly that the object he has in view is to give the working classes a better share in the advantages and the blessings of civilisation, which are so largely the results of their labour. Not only have they a right to generous education, and to free enjoyment of the agencies of culture possessed by the nation, but they can justly claim a higher degree of material welfare,—in other words, a larger share in the national income. How is the latter to be secured ? There are two ways in which the desired end may be reached. (1) The workman may benefit by the increasing productivity of national labour. This, however, would at best be a slow and uncertain process, and Wagner advocates a more effective method of raising the position of the working-man. (2) Labour may benefit at the expense of capital—the lower classes may benefit at the expense of the higher—by the latter giving to the labourer better remuneration, higher wages, which implies the reduction of profit, interest, and rent in their various forms. Wagner's position differs from that of the Socialists in that they would abolish social inequalities, while he would only seek to diminish them. He makes no concealment of the fact that he proposes to take from the rich for the benefit of the poor. The rich might complain of this, but it would not be with reason.

---

[1] " Rede über die sociale Frage," pp. 8 and 9.

" What would be taken from the higher classes the workman has hitherto had to do without, with far greater hardship than his more privileged fellow-man would in future experience through its loss, for his position would still remain far better than the labourer's."

Coming now to Wagner's demands in detail, he requires in the industrial domain that wages shall be increased, so that a higher standard of life may be maintained; that the hours of work shall be reduced, so that a workman's physical strength may be econo-mised and leisure be afforded for mental improvement and rational enjoyment; and that Sunday labour shall be abolished, in the interest of morality and religion. He would not object to the State regulating the hours of labour, to the extent of fixing a maxi-mum work-day, but he thinks Boards of Arbitration and Labour Chambers better fitted to deal with the question. Hand in hand with the regulation of the hours of labour would go the exercise of a strict supervision over the conditions of labour, which, both from the sanitary and the moral standpoint, should be such as to shield both mind and body from deleterious influence. Naturally the industrial insurance laws now in operation in Germany have Wagner's approval; indeed, years before their inception he called for laws affording to the working classes maintenance in times of sickness, accident, and old age. The "wages-contract" should also be an equitable one, and measures should be devised for securing to the workman continuous employment as far as possible; the least the State can do is to ensure the giving of ample notice in case of employment ceasing. Wagner favours co-operation in distribution on the basis of the English co-operative movement, and also, to some extent, in production. Having derived Social-istic stimulus from Rodbertus and Lassalle, we need not wonder that he should advocate the productive partnership for working-men, making the labourer at once the undertaker, the workman at once the capitalist. Indeed, he goes so far as to say that Lassalle's proposal of State credit might with advantage be adopted. At the same time he admits that practical objections exist, such as the difficulties of organisation, of administration, of exercising the State control which would be necessary, and of regulating the rela-tions between the various undertakings carried on with State funds.

In a work published a number of years ago he, however, suggested that an experiment might be made in this direction by the State converting some of its mines and smelting works into industrial partnerships, broadly hinting that in the event of a successful result being achieved it might not be out of the question to compulsorily convert private undertakings into co-operative concerns. All Wagner's proposals in this domain proceed from the desire to improve the workman's lot by restricting the capitalist's power over him, which also implies the restriction of the capitalist's power over his own means of production.

But the working classes can be helped in other ways, and one is by lightening their taxation. Wagner strongly favours indirect taxes, but he stipulates that the objects of taxation should be such as lightly touch the labourer. Thus the taxes and duties on corn, beer, sugar, tea, coffee, salt, and upon dwellings should be kept within moderate bounds. On the other hand, the luxuries of the rich may be taxed liberally. As regards direct taxation, the labourer's income should, as far as possible, be exempted, and the well-to-do classes should pay proportionately more. In taxing income, however, a distinction should be drawn between the income derived from business and personal service, which should be lightly dealt with, and funded income, proceeding from land and investments, which should be highly taxed. Taxation should also be progressive, whatever the source of income. Wagner would allow the national treasury to share more liberally in dead men's gold. If the State sees that a legator's heirs receive their own, it should be well recompensed for its service. He proposes a legacy tax progressive according to the distance of relationship and also according to the extent of the bequest. Distant relatives he is prepared to disqualify in favour of the State. Wagner further proposes to tax unearned increment heavily, as will be shown, and to make income derived from Stock Exchange speculation and gambling pay a high tribute to the public treasury.

It is, however, in his proposals regarding real estate of all kinds that Wagner's views, both as to taxation and State intervention, betray the truest stamp of State Socialism. He approaches very near to the theories of acquired right laid down by Savigny and Lassalle when he says that in every contract affecting property an

expropriation clause should be implied, its exercise depending
upon the will and requirements of society. Like Savigny, but
unlike Lassalle,[1] he would give fair compensation in case of dis-
possession. Wagner and Samter [2] are equally emphatic in opposing the idea of absolute right in the possession of land. Unlike
the products of man's hand, land cannot be multiplied. So much
exists, and labour is powerless to create more. Being thus a
monopoly article, and at the same time the great productive force
in nature and the maintainer of life, individual interests should be
rigidly subordinated to social in all economic and legal institutions affecting the land. Private possession should not be excluded, but State and collective possession is both allowable and
desirable; and expediency and experience should dictate which
categories of property should be handed over to the individual,
which reserved for society, and which be possessed by both conjointly. Wagner holds that the State or public bodies may wisely
and beneficially possess the following kinds of real estate :—

1. They should unconditionally possess the forests, both for
climatic and fiscal reasons. In Germany more than one-half of
the forest-land is already in public hands, and some of the States
derive a large part of their revenues from the domains. If the
State or the parish retains its lands, the public, and not private
owners, will reap the benefit of the unearned increment created by
social causes. When Hanover was annexed by Prussia the leases
of the domain lands were readjusted, and many were raised from
40 to 120 per cent. This increased return went to the diminution
of public taxation.

2. As to agricultural land, Wagner prefers that small estates
should be in private hands, but private ownership cannot be
unconditionally conceded in the case of large estates. The
accumulation of land in few hands has the tendency to minimise

---

[1] Lassalle's argument is that "every age is independent and autonomous,"
that the customs, traditions, and precedents of the past cannot claim absolute
validity in the present. A right exists only so long as society wills that it shall
exist. See his clever "System der erworbenen Rechte " (Leipzig, 1861, 2
vols.).

[2] See Wagner's *Lehrbuch*, and his "Rede über die sociale Frage," and
Samter's "Das Eigenthum in seiner sozialen Bedeutung" (Jena, 1879), and
his "Eigenthumsbegriff" (Jena, 1878).

its public usefulness. A relatively greater number of persons are supported on small estates than on large ones. Thus Wagner claims for the State the right to expropriate great owners in favour of peasant proprietors.

3. Private property in urban land is very dangerous, as it leads to unhealthy and immoral speculation and to the exploitation of society by purse-proud landlords. Owing to the existence of a monopoly, the price of land is forced to a fictitious height, rents are excessive, and speculative builders and house-owners wax rich on the industry and progress of the inhabitants whom their bricks and plaster shelter. Wagner holds that speculation in building-land is "an economically unjustifiable and morally unpermissible misuse of the rights of property." In order to put an end to it, he would transfer urban house property from private to public hands. He proposes two ways of doing this. Either local authorities might acquire both land and buildings and supply all future residential wants themselves, or the State might acquire the land and the local authorities the buildings. By this means society would be effectively protected from the plundering instincts of the speculator, and would enjoy all the future spontaneous value of land. So long, however, as urban land continues in private hands, Wagner would, by a well-devised system of taxation, based on periodical valuations, give to the community a share in the unearned increment. This is also one of Samter's principal proposals.

4. Means of communication, such as roads, railways, and canals, should belong to the State or public bodies—railways and canals unconditionally to the State. The purpose of railways should be utilitarian rather than financial. The railway may not properly be made a dividend-creator; its end is public convenience. If the railways are nationalised, speculation—which Wagner invariably condemns in unsparing terms as both a social and an ethical evil—is prevented, the exploitation of the public is impossible, and whatever financial benefit may accrue from this property will go to society. Various advantages are also claimed for a nationalised railway system, such as uniformity and economy of administration, strategic importance, etc.

5. Finally, Wagner favours State and collective possession in

the case of mines where the products are found in a usable condition, as coal and salt. Coal especially, as the "bread of industry," should be in collective possession.[1] The same cannot, however, be claimed for ore mines, for here labour plays a great part, and these may with advantage be left in private hands.

Wagner further demands that the State shall be allowed to take part in production in domains which the individualist would carefully reserve to private enterprise. He even goes to the extent of State monopoly, as in the cases of brandy and tobacco. Here not only fiscal reasons have weight with him ; he holds that it would be to the interest of consumers if the State took in hand the production of these articles, in which, as at present carried on, there is notoriously a large amount of adulteration and dishonesty, against which the public cannot protect itself. Insurance is another suitable field for State activity, and he is prepared to extend public insurance not only to life and person (accident, death, old age, etc.), but to movable property. Proposals regarding the latter were some time ago introduced in the Bavarian and Saxon Diets, their authors desiring to establish State competitive establishments. The constitution, however (by article 4), reserves the subject of insurance for imperial legislation and supervision, and the project could not be seriously considered. The advantages claimed by Wagner for public insurance are : (1) that there would be better security; and (2) that the system would be cheaper and more economical, as it would not be necessary to make profits to be distributed in dividends.

Such, in brief, are the leading ideas embodied in Wagner's theoretical scheme of State Socialism.[2] Many of his critics object that his State Socialism is in reality Socialism pure and simple, or would be if developed to logical conclusions. "Certainly," says

---

[1] Is it out of place to ask here how long it will be before our British Parliament thinks it necessary to inquire into the tenability of the non-intervention principle which allows the coal supplies of Great Britain to be depleted, in the interest of foreign countries, to the extent of millions of tons a year, through exports which, after all, bring a modicum of profit ? Can it be accounted an economic fallacy to restrict freedom of trade abroad by law, when the article exported is a *natural product*, limited in extent, yet of incalculable value to the present generation and the future ?

[2] See Appendix A for Wagner's State Socialistic programme.

one of these commentators—one of the friendly group, for no living German economist has been treated to more of the gall and wormwood of perverse animadversion than Professor Wagner— "there is no fear of Wagner losing himself in the excesses of Social-Democracy, but his moderation does not lie in the consequence of his standpoint." It cannot be denied that Wagner has cast entirely away the economic shibboleths of the time. His whole attitude is a protest against the fallacy of finality in economic doctrines and institutions, and it says much for his strength of conviction that he should have placed himself at the head of a bold and daring rebellion against the old order of economic Liberalism when State intervention was not a popular phrase.

Even now Wagner is far ahead of most scientific State Socialists, and of its representatives in the sphere of practical legislation. Time alone can show whether he has accurately gauged the tendencies of the times. It is significant, however, that the doctrines of State Socialism are now far less controverted in Germany than a few years ago. The main principles are granted ; and the economic and political parties which not long ago were found opposing the reaction against the prevailing Liberalistic order of things, now at best endeavour to keep the new movement within moderate bounds. The remarkable social legislation passed during the declining years of the Emperor William has undoubtedly done much to popularise this movement, and it is safe to predict that the reforms already introduced will yet be followed by many others, if not of equal moment, still conceived in the same spirit. To use the words of a warm friend of the modern social developments of Germany : "So much is certain : State Socialism is the soul which pervades the entire imperial legislation of to-day. It has already become an article of faith, and is now a constituent of the mental atmosphere in which the present lives and breathes."

CHAPTER II.

THUS far we have seen the theoretical side of State Socialism. An important characteristic of this economical system is its recognition of the national idea. As State Socialism is the protest of Collectivism against Individualism, so it is the protest of Nationality against Cosmopolitanism. It proceeds from the axiom that the first duty of the State is to maintain and promote the interests, the well-being of the nation as such. Next in importance, however, to this duty, is the duty of affording help and protection to the subjects of the State according to their necessities. Not only have all citizens to be secured in the possession of their rights, but the weaker classes of the community have a claim to preferential consideration, the State regarding it as its business to help them when they cannot help themselves. Already the theory of State Socialism has received wide application in Germany ; but as in legislation theory always keeps far in advance of practice, much remains to be done before the scientific exponents of this system will be satisfied. The departments of State Socialism in which legislation has so far been especially active include the following :—

(1) Factory and general industrial laws :
  (*a*) Hours of labour.
  (*b*) Conditions of labour.
  (*c*) Special laws for women and children.
  (*d*) Insurance of workpeople.
(2) Commercial protection (customs duties).
(3) Taxation.
(4) Promotion of colonisation and trade.
(5) State undertakings :
  (*a*) Railways.
  (*b*) Monopolies.

It will never be possible to understand and appreciate the State Socialistic measures adopted in Germany since the establishment of the new Empire, unless they are considered in relation to the past social-political policy of Prussia. No mistake could be greater, and yet none is more common amongst the observers of Prince Bismarck's imperial legislation, than the idea that State Socialism is a new thing in Germany, a purely modern growth owing its origin to accident or the temporary exigencies of a perplexed statesman. To those who regard State Socialism in this light, the series of social, industrial, and commercial measures which the last twenty years have called forth in Germany must indeed seem remarkable, if not inexplicable. But continuity of legislation is as natural to Germany as it is to England, and instead of denoting a completely new departure in economics, these measures are in reality but a continuation of, or a reversion to, traditional policy. Prince Bismarck has done nothing more than develop the social and political system established by the Great Elector, Frederick William I., and Frederick the Great of Prussia. He has taken up the threads of policy which were laid down when, after the Liberation War, the laws of Stein and Hardenberg —passed to meet pressing necessities—gave practical expression to Free Trade and Individualistic ideas, and has endeavoured to infuse the spirit of the old Prussian Monarchy into the new German Empire. How this has been done will be seen as we consider the various measures which have united to characterise the last twenty years of German legislation as emphatically an era of State Socialism.

It was the attachment of the reigning house to the idea of nationality, its constant endeavour to promote justice between man and man, and its solicitude for the welfare of the poorer classes which led to the unbounded popularity of the Hohenzollerns amongst their people, whose loyalty to king and crown never varied amid the trying vicissitudes of Prussian history during the seventeenth and eighteenth centuries. The Prussian monarchy differs from other European monarchies in many things, but especially in its traditionally democratic sympathies. It was the proud boast of the Great Frederick that he was *"le roi des gueux;"* and solicitude first for the prosperity and welfare of the nation as a whole, and then in an especial degree for the happiness of the weaker classes, has always been the key-note of Prussian kingly policy. Thus has been generated a popular attachment to the Crown which in the political convulsions of 1789, not less than in the ferment of forty years ago, proved strong enough to resist every strain.

We see the State Socialistic idea first taking distinct form in the legislation and more still the royal decrees and ordinances of Frederick the Great. Under him the "police state" approached its ideal realisation. Adopting as his motto, "*Salus publica, suprema lex,*" he endeavoured in home government to hold the scales of justice evenly, to administer with efficiency and economy, and to protect the weak against the strong by checking the ascendency of the aristocracy. During his reign the mercantile theory was supreme. All economic measures had as their end the creation of a national state. In connection with his Government, he established a department for commerce and manufactures, and the royal instructions issued to this office were most numerous and various. Native industries and native trade were protected and stimulated, not only by the imposition of import duties, but by premiums on exports and by the direct subsidising of struggling manufactures.

The King himself established industrial undertakings, not for purposes of revenue, but for his country's enrichment. At one time (June, 1783) he devoted 260,000 thalers from his own purse to the reform of the Prussian mining and smelting system. Industries were also encouraged by the granting of commercial privileges, by the import by the State of raw materials, which were re-sold at low prices, and by premiums upon technical improvements. The guilds were, moreover, made powerless to hinder industrial progress, roads and canals were built, a State post was introduced, and in many other ways the commercial instincts of the nation were stimulated. To the enterprise of Frederick the Great are to be attributed the Plauen, Finow, Swine, and Bromberg canals, the harbour and town of Swinemünde, and other great works. Where industries did not exist, Frederick introduced them. Handicraftsmen of various kinds were induced to leave Holland and France and settle in Prussia, to which country they brought valuable technical knowledge, the results of which were soon seen in new and thriving industries. In 1786, the year of Frederick's death, no fewer than a third of the inhabitants of Prussia are said to have been immigrants or the descendants of immigrants. Measures were taken to build up a foreign trade. Commercial treaties were concluded with a number of countries, including Turkey, Persia, Holland, and the United States, to this end; and we find towards the end of the eighteenth century an extensive export of textile, iron, steel, brass, bronze, and leather goods from Prussia. Foreign trading adventures were assisted, as the Emdener Handelscompagnie (1751) and the Seehandlungscompagnie (1772), the latter connected since 1848 with the Prussian Ministry of Finance. As to the general economic policy of the early Prussian sovereigns, and especially of Frederick the Great, an authoritative writer says :—

"The Electors of Brandenburg from the earliest times devoted special attention to the economic circumstances of their territories. Many of the decrees issued went, it is true, far beyond the mark, and did not attain the desired result. Here, as elsewhere, where territorial sovereignty had developed strength, the paternal system had reached its highest development, and the Government regulated the smallest and greatest matters alike. . . . Of all Governments of those days (17th century), the Prussian was the first to seek the welfare of the whole community. Every energy was directed to this end. It was the duty of the monarch to 'keep ever on the watch,' as the great king (Frederick) expressed it later. . . . The work of national reorganisation, in the narrowest sense of the word, is a great merit of the Great Elector. In order to populate wasted districts, he attracted foreigners to the country. Agriculture revived, and industry developed in particular through the immigration of French Huguenots, to whom houses, land, and freedom from taxation were granted for several years, and who were given financial support. . . .

"The endeavours of Frederick the Great to improve the economic condition of Prussia cannot be sufficiently estimated, even though one may not agree with the fundamental ideas by which he was led. He gave equal attention to trade, industry, and agriculture. By inducing foreigners to settle down in various provinces,

he sought to give to agriculture the labour required in the drain-
ing of marshy districts and the cultivation of waste lands.   .   .   .
Numerous decrees prove the care with which the King promoted
agricultural interests ; better methods came into application, and
the instruction given to the peasants at the command of the King
had very successful results. . . . Worthy of all admiration is the
energy of the King, who repeatedly enjoined his subjects to plant
vacant lands with fruit-trees, to lay out hop-gardens, and to cultivate the vine, flax, madder, woad, caraway-seed, anise-seed, etc.
It was, however, a great evil that, owing to the opposition of the
nobility, the King was not able to abolish serfage, hereditary servitude, etc., and that he had to be satisfied with the amelioration
of the peasants' oppressed condition." [1]

Under Frederick William II., Prussian *prestige*, both politically
and commercially, suffered a great blow.   There have been kings
of Prussia who have gone to extravagance in the pursuit of their
ideals, but this is the only king who has had no ideal.   The impetus given in the preceding reign to industry and trade still,
however, continued a beneficial influence, until dark days set in
for Prussia, and with the Napoleonic era her star of fortune
passed into eclipse.

In Prussia the State Socialistic idea has in no department of
public policy been more conspicuous than in poor relief and care
for the welfare of the working classes.   When Frederick the
Great was asked to sanction a tax on meat and bread, he returned
the official document containing the request with the note : " I
will never agree to make the poor man's bread and meat dearer ;
I am the advocate of the poor ; " and the same spirit characterised
his successors, without exception.

But the Prussian common law, as promulgated by Frederick
William II. in 1794, went farther than the voluntary clemency of
the Crown.   This law was drawn up during several reigns.   Begun
by the Elector Johann Georg (1571–1598), the work was continued by the Elector Frederick William and King Frederick
William I., and was completed by Frederick William II., coming

---

[1] "Allgemeine Geschichte des Welthandels" (Adolf Beer), 2te Abthei-
lung, p. 457 *et seq.*

into force July 1st, 1794. The Prussian *Landrecht* discourages idleness, recognises the right of every citizen to work, and proclaims the State to be the natural protector of the poorer classes. It contains the following clauses :—

1. It is the duty of the State to provide for the sustenance and support of those of its citizens who cannot . . . procure subsistence themselves.

2. Work adapted to their strength and capacities shall be supplied to those who lack means and opportunity of earning a livelihood for themselves and those dependent upon them.

3. Those who, from laziness, love of idleness, or other irregular proclivities, do not choose to employ the means offered them of earning a livelihood, shall be kept to useful work by compulsion and punishment under proper control.

6. The State is entitled and is bound to take such measures as will prevent the destitution of its citizens and check excessive extravagance.

15. The police authority of every place must provide for all poor and destitute persons, whose subsistence cannot be ensured in any other way.

It was upon these clauses that Prince Bismarck relied when on May 9th, 1884, he declared to the Reichstag his recognition of the labourer's " Right to work " (" *Recht auf Arbeit* ").

Another and still more important State measure for the amelioration of the lower orders of the people is seen in the Stein-Hardenberg legislation which followed the Liberation Wars. This series of reforms emancipated the land, abolished feudal privileges, established a free peasant proprietary, reformed the guild system, repealed excessive duties and excises, and made taxation more equal by introducing the principle of taxation according to individual ability. The measures of Stein were condemned in his day, but now they receive nothing but approbation. In Bavaria a movement towards social reform was made as early as 1808, when serfage was abolished, and the agrarian laws in general were softened. But no great advance was made, and the Crown could only be induced to take reforms in hand seriously when the revolution of 1848 broke out. After Stein and Hardenberg, a period of reaction followed. The ideas of the individualistic school gained ascendency; free competition and free trade became the political shibboleths of the day, and the police State of the eighteenth century fell into ill-repute.

The first impulse was given to the Free Trade movement in Prussia by the legislation of 1818. In old Germany there was no uniform economic policy. The country being divided into a great number of States, each with its own laws and customs, national action in the domain of economics was impossible. What actually existed was a system of mutual destruction. Each State believed that its commercial prosperity required the adoption of stringent protective measures against its neighbours. High and often insurmountable customs barriers divided populations whose interests were in reality identical. Not only were duties imposed on imports, but prohibitive imposts frequently prevented the possibility of exportation. All countries suffered by this international war of tariffs. The Stein-Hardenberg reforms did much to relieve the industry and trade of Prussia from obstacles which impeded their progress. They aimed at protecting and encouraging home manufactures. Internal duties were abolished, but frontier duties were maintained. The law of May 26th, 1818, stated : "The duties shall, by an expedient taxation of foreign trade and of the consumption of foreign goods, afford protection to home industry, and secure to the State the revenue which trade and luxury can yield without obstructing commerce." Henceforth there were no more prohibitions and monopolies save the State monopolies of salt and playing-cards. The export trade was less restricted, though the direct support of industry by the State ceased. The principle of the free admission of raw material, established by Frederick the Great, was maintained, but moderate duties were imposed on half-manufactured materials. Eight years before this, freedom in the choice and exercise of handicraft was decreed by the edict of November 2nd, 1810.

On the whole, the measure of 1818 marked a clear departure from ancient policy. It was in letter as well as in spirit the reversal of the economic principles of the Great Frederick, who may *par excellence* be called the founder of Prussian industry and commerce.

Prince Bismarck was right when he told the Reichstag on June 14th, 1882, that the protective system was but "a reversion to the traditional Prussian policy. Under Frederick the Great there was a greater degree of protection than under the *Zollverein*, and the attempt to break with protection was only a modern innovation." So general was the opinion that, with the passing of the law of 1818, Prussia had declared herself on the side of Free Trade, that the English economist William Huskisson could assert in that year that Prussian policy was a pattern to England and the world.

Upon the basis of Prussia's new protective tariff was founded the *Zollverein*, a commercial union of German States, the centre and soul of which was Prussia. Other slighter combinations preceded it, but having no cohesion they were dissolved. The principle of the union was the abolition of duties within the territory it comprised. Import duties were levied on the frontiers of that territory, and the revenue thus raised was divided amongst the contracting States in accordance with their several populations.

In 1834 the *Zollverein* comprised eighteen States, and its territory extended to 7,719 square miles, and had a population of twenty-three millions ; and two years later, with the addition of Hesse-Homburg, Baden, Nassau, and Frankfort, its extent was increased to 8,252 square miles, and its population to over twenty-five millions. When the treaty was for the second time prolonged in 1854, all the German States except Austria, the two Mecklenburgs, and the Hanseatic Cities belonged to the union. The association of so many States in a commercial alliance naturally entailed great divergence of views on economical questions. For a time, however, the Free Trade spirit continued supreme, and up to 1840 the tendency was to reduce the duties levied on imports. In 1819 Friedrich List established the " Deutscher Handels- und Gewerbeverein " ("German Commercial and Industrial Association "), whose policy was freedom of trade at home with reciprocity for foreign rivals, and this organisation fairly represented the prevailing feeling. After 1840 more protection became the rule, and many duties were increased twofold, threefold, and even fourfold. This tendency to greater protection continued until the conclusion of commercial treaties with France and England early in the sixties.   In 1865 a new tariff was adopted repealing many duties and reducing others.   Further reductions took place in 1868, 1869, 1873, and 1877, in which last year the remaining duties on iron were abolished.   At this time the policy of Germany—now become a unified Empire—was distinctly a Free Trade policy.

CHAPTER III.

BISMARCK'S SOCIAL PRINCIPLES.

IT has already been said that the State Socialistic legislation of the German Empire cannot properly be appreciated unless it be considered in relation to the traditional economic policy of Prussia, upon which it is based. Similarly, in examining the attitude of Prince Bismarck, who more than any other man has been instrumental in bringing that legislation into existence, it is necessary to know the standpoints from which he has proceeded. In other words, what are Bismarck's ideas concerning society and the State? How does he interpret their duties, one to the other? What is the ideal at which his social-political policy aims? These questions must be answered if we are to do justice to the German Chancellor's efforts on behalf of social amelioration. The idea that Prince Bismarck purposes the re-establishment of the old despotic monarchy may at once be dismissed as absurd. He is again and again charged with dark political designs, but neither his public sayings nor his ministerial acts afford justification for the imputation. His aims are social rather than political. He has, it is true, created a reaction, but the reaction is economic : it is, moreover, a reaction against a reaction—the reaction of Collectivism following that of Individualism.

Prince Bismarck proceeds from the proposition that the State is a Christian institution. So long ago as June 15th, 1847, he declared to the Prussian United Diet, which was not accustomed to hear such words from an obscure provincial deputy :—

"I am of opinion that the idea of the Christian State is as old as the *ci-devant* Holy Roman Empire, as old as all the European States, that it is the soil in which these States have taken root, and that a State, if it would have an assured permanence, if it would only justify its existence, when it is disputed, must stand on a religious foundation. . . . I believe I am right in calling that State a Christian State which seeks to realise the teaching of Christianity. That our State has not succeeded in doing this in all respects was shown yesterday by the Deputy Baron von Vincke in a parallel, more ingenious than agreeable to my religious feelings, between the truths of the Gospel and the paragraphs of the common law."

More than a generation later he gave expression to the same views in the Reichstag. On April 2nd, 1881, he said :—

" I should like to see the State, which for the most part consists of Christians—although you reject the name Christian State—penetrated to some extent by the principles of the religion it professes ; especially as concerns the help one gives to his neighbour, and sympathy with the lot of old and suffering people."

Again, he has said, when justifying his social measures : " If a name be desired for our endeavours which I could willingly accept, it is practical Christianity, but *sans phrase.*" Yet again, on January 9th, 1882, he said :—

" I do not comprehend with what right we acknowledge the commands of Christianity as binding upon our private dealings, and yet in the most important sphere of our duty—participation in the legislation of a country having a population of forty-five million people—push them into the background and say, here we need not trouble. For my part I confess openly that my belief in the consequence of our revealed religion, in the form of moral law, is sufficient for me, and certainly for the position taken up on this question by the Emperor, and that the question of the Christian or non-Christian State has nothing to do with the matter. I, the minister of the State, am a Christian, and as such I am determined to act as I believe I am justified before God."

Entertaining such an idea of the State, it can cause no surprise to say that Prince Bismarck's social policy is largely prompted by religious motives. The State, regarded as the executive power, exists for the benefit of all. It is the duty of the State to see that the social organism is preserved in a healthy condition. This can only be possible when all classes of society act upon the principles of mutual obligation, mutual dependence, and mutual help. So long as these principles lie at the foundation of national life, all will go well. If, on the other hand, they are disregarded,—

if antipathy takes the place of sympathy,—if there is neglect of social obligations, the mechanism of society cannot work smoothly. The deduction from this proposition is, that when social inequalities exist, the State, as the organ responsible for the ordered movement of national life, must intervene in the interest of conciliation, peace, and progress. The position of Prince Bismarck, shortly stated, is this : upon the citizens of the State are imposed social duties, and it is the business of the State to see that they are faithfully discharged.

As a critic, one of his countrymen, has well said, he regards the present constitution of society as in its foundations right and unassailable, and he accepts them as natural and necessary. "Rich and poor, capitalist and labourer, are to him categories of actual necessity." But as there must be rich and poor, he preaches to the rich the duty of love for their neighbours ; and as they often omit to do their duty voluntarily, he compels them by means of the State.[1]

How completely national and truly popular are Prince Bismarck's sympathies and aims is shown best, of course, by the social legislation which is associated with his direction of imperial policy since 1871 ; but his early and later speeches contain frequent reference to the objects of his statescraft. He told the Reichstag on February 24th, 1881 :—

" For me there has been but one compass, one pole-star, after which I have steered: *Salus publica.* Since I entered public life I have often, perhaps, acted rashly and imprudently. But when I have had time for reflection I have always been guided by the question,—what is most beneficial, most expedient, and proper for my dynasty so long as I was only in Prussia, and nowadays for the German nation ? I have never in my life been *doctrinaire.* All systems by which parties are divided and bound together are of secondary moment to me. My first thought is of the nation, its position abroad, its independence, our organisation in such a way that we may breathe freely in the world."

We shall be prepared to find Bismarck a law unto himself, to see

[1] Franz Stöpel: "Die Wirthschafts- und Sozialpolitik des Fürsten Bismarck," Leipzig, 1885.

him rebelling against orthodoxy, making light of musty traditions, shaking himself free from the cobwebs of custom and conventionalism, turning rudely upon party creeds and shibboleths, and even behaving to science with irreverence. Again and again he has hushed his academic critics with the rough and ready argument, " No theory ! " He prefers to judge of society as he sees it and knows it, and not according to principles and *formulæ* laid down in books. With him an ounce of fact is worth a ton of theory ; an actually existing fly worth the best of possibly existing angels. Practical common-sense and experience of men and the world have ever been his guides in social politics, as well as in the higher reaches of statesmanship. If science agrees with experience, so much the better for science ; if it does not agree, so much the worse, for it must go to the wall. " In all these questions " (of economics), he said in the Reichstag, May 2nd, 1879, when advocating reform in the customs system, " I pay as little regard to science as I do in any other judgment of organic institutions. Our surgery has made splendid progress during the last two thousand years ; but medical science has made no progress in regard to the internal conditions of the body, into which the human eye cannot see, and here we stand face to face with the same riddles as before. So it is with the organic formation of States. In this respect the abstract doctrines of science do not influence me : I judge according to the experience which we have. I see that the countries which protect themselves prosper, that the countries which are open are declining, and that great and powerful England, that strong combatant, who, after strengthening her muscles, entered the market and said : ' Who will contest with me ? I am ready for any one,' is gradually going back to protective duties, and will in a few years adopt them so far as is necessary to preserving at least the English market."

Again, on February 10th, 1885, he said : " With mere learning, with exact and irrefutable argumentation, we do not make any progress in this domain. It is like medical advice upon internal diseases : it must always be liable to errors, and there I should not trust my own judgment, and the judgment of another but little more."

His independence of judgment and his impatience of anything

approaching shibboleth have often served Bismarck in good stead in the course of his parliamentary career. "Since I became minister," he once said, "I have never belonged to a fraction, nor could I." He has accepted allies wherever he could find them, now suffering his measures to be carried to success on the backs of Liberals, now on those of Conservatives. It would hardly be fair to speak of him as a man of expedients, yet he has declared that "the basis of constitutional life is everywhere compromise." Entering public life the sincere admirer and defender of Prussian State principles and institutions as he found them—he declared in the Prussian United Diet, June 15th, 1847 : "I grant that I am full of prejudices ; I sucked them in with my mother's milk, and I cannot possibly argue them away"—he has had to abandon many a cherished notion, to turn upon and rend many a dear conviction of his younger days.

There was a time when he warmly opposed the granting of equal civil rights to the Jews, and when he denounced in Parliament the institution of civil marriage as a materialistic fallacy, dangerous alike to religion and the State. Yet his early anti-Semitic prejudices did not prevent him from extending later a full measure of tolerance to the Hebrew part of the population, and his denunciation of the civil marriage in 1849 was not allowed to stand in the way of the legalisation of that institution in Prussia in 1873, though the measure was the result of necessity rather than of conviction and preference. Bismarck's position in these and similar matters affecting the organisation of the State was explained to the Prussian Diet on April 10th, 1875, when he laid it down as a political maxim that a nation's constitution should follow the changes which take place in the national life, being so modified as to keep in constant accord with these changes.

Bismarck's success as a statesman and a legislator has been great, but all his genius, all his sound common-sense, all his conciliation would have served him ill had he not been inspired by a resolution and a dogged perseverance which recognised no impossibility. Given clear conviction upon a question and a decided line of action, and no opposition could daunt him. "Whether I suffer defeats or not," he told the Reichstag on July 9th, 1879, "whether I have to begin at the beginning or not, so long as I remain minister I shall not relax my endeavours. My prototype is Robert Bruce in the story of the spider, whose repeated re-climbing after falling down encouraged him not to abandon that which he regarded as right and as advantageous for the fatherland, however unpropitious his prospects. But the prospects of the measures which I have undertaken are not bad or discouraging, and in my opinion it would be treachery to the cause which I represent here in the name of the Fatherland, and which I have not frivolously espoused, if I allowed such trivialities as those which distinguish one theory from the other to prevent me from attaining my goal at a moment when I might stretch my hand out to it." Even more impressive are the words which he used in the same place on February 4th, 1881 : "I will not swerve one hair's-breadth. When I am tired, I will rest ; but I will not turn back, but will die in the breach—if God please, perhaps, one day in this very place if I may live no longer."

So much for the fundamental principles which underlie Prince Bismarck's legislation, and for the rules and tactics which have guided him in the practical business of creating parliamentary majorities. What we now know of the man will better enable us to appreciate his work.

The legislation of the State Socialistic era will receive necessary treatment in succeeding chapters. Here it is only needful to indicate its principal characteristics. From first to last it is a protest against Individualism, against *Laissez-faire.* Prince Bismarck has dispersed to the four winds of heaven the old doctrine that the State has nothing to do with economics. The Progressists, who have in the Reichstag and the Prussian Diet dis-puted every foot of the ground he has covered by social-political legislation, still maintain that they are right after all, and that State meddling in economical affairs is unjustifiable. Prince Bismarck, meanwhile, makes his opponents a present of science and theory, and quietly pursues his forward way. He holds that the State has far more to do, if it would discharge its duty to society, than act as a sort of military patrol. Preservation of peace without and within is all well enough so far as it goes, but the province of government does not end there. The State has not only to see that its subjects live in concord, but to take care that, so far as may be possible, their social conditions are such as promote contentment and happiness. Thus beyond and above the duty of securing citizens in the possession of their rights is the duty of determining what rights may properly be secured to the individual. The State's functions are thus not passive but active. On this subject Prince Bismarck once expressed himself very forcibly in the Reichstag when answering the criticisms of the Progressist leader. He said :—

"Herr Richter has called attention to the responsibility of the State for what it does. But it is my opinion that the State can also be responsible for what it does not do. I do not think that doctrines like those of '*Laissez-faire, laissez-aller,*' 'Pure Manchesterdom in politics,' '*Jeder sehe, wie er's treibe, Jeder sehe, wo er bleibe,*' [1] 'He who is not strong enough to stand must be knocked down and trodden to the ground,' 'To him that hath shall be given, and from him that hath not shall be taken away even that which he hath,'—that doctrines like these should be applied in the State, and especially in a monarchically, paternally governed State. On the other hand, I believe that those who profess horror at the intervention of the State for the protection of the weak lay themselves open to the suspicion that they are desirous of using their strength—be it that of capital, that of rhetoric, or whatever it be—for the benefit of a section, for the oppression of the rest, for the introduction of party domination, and that they will be chagrined as soon as this design is disturbed by any action of the Government."

More than a decade before Prince Bismarck inaugurated his social-political legislation, he had, as Prussian Minister President, exerted his official influence in favour of State, or at any rate Crown, help for the working classes. When in England in 1862 he was struck with the magnitude and the success of the co-

---

[1] From Goethe's "Zahme Xenien" :—

> "Eines schickt sich nicht für Alle !
> Sehe Jeder, wie er's treibe,
> Sehe Jeder, wo er bleibe,
> Und wer steht, dass er nicht falle."

A prose rendering would be : "The same thing is not suited to all. Let every one care for himself, and let he who is standing take heed that he do not fall."

operative system, and the result of his inquiries into the working of Productive Associations in this country was that on his return home he persuaded the Prussian king to expend a considerable sum of money on experiments in the same direction. The experiments had not a fair trial, for owing to political causes they had soon to be abandoned. Ferdinand Lassalle was at this time agitating Prussia on behalf of his projected " Universal German Working-Men's Association ; " and Prince Bismarck admits not only having been favourably drawn to the idea of co-operative production on some such lines as those advocated by this Association, but having taken counsel with the Socialist leader not once but several times.[1] Nothing came of his contact with Lassalle, so far as the latter's great scheme of State-supported Productive Associations was concerned, but a short time later Bismarck induced the King of Prussia to advance money to a body of Silesian weavers, to enable them to establish a co-operative manufactory. This incident deserves more than passing mention. Several hundred weavers in 1865 petitioned to be heard at the throne through three of their number, and the Minister President obtained the desired audience. The men belonged to the Wüstegiersdorf district, which is situated in a mountainous part of Silesia, and it was proved that their condition had long been very lamentable, owing to their precarious employment and to the harshness of their employers. The average workman, labouring twelve hours a day, was only able to earn by great diligence the trifle of 3*s.* 6*d.* a week, and those who were most skilled and who had the best work only earned 3*s.* more. Bismarck saw here an opportunity of putting the co-operative principle to the test, and the Silesian weavers were supplied with funds from the royal purse. As usual the Pro-

---

[1] Bismarck referred as follows to his relations with Lassalle in a speech delivered in the Reichstag on April 2nd, 1881 : " Lassalle himself wanted urgently to enter into negotiations with me, and if I could find time to search among old papers I believe I could yet find the letter in which the wish is expressed, and reasons are given why I should allow the wish to be fulfilled. Nor did I make it difficult for Lassalle to meet me. I saw him, and from the time that I first spoke an hour with him I have not regretted it." Bismarck has also left it on record that his conversations with Lassalle ranged over the entire field of social politics.

gressist members of the Prussian Diet had a good deal to say on the matter, and the action of the minister was roundly condemned. In his reply to animadversions, Bismarck said :—

"I ask you what right had I to close the way to the throne against these people ? The kings of Prussia have never been by preference kings of the rich. Frederick the Great said when Crown Prince : '*Quand je serai roi, je serai un vrai roi des gueux.*' He undertook to be the protector of the poor, and this principle has been followed by our later kings. At their throne suffering has always found a refuge and a hearing. . . .

"Our kings have secured the emancipation of the serfs, they have created a thriving peasantry, and they may possibly be successful—the earnest endeavour exists, at any rate—in improving the condition of the working classes somewhat. To have refused access to the throne to the complaints of these operatives would not have been the right course to pursue, and it was, moreover, not my business to do it. The question would afterwards have been asked: 'How rich must a deputation be in order to its reception by the King?'" As for the granting of royal money to the distressed weavers, Bismarck could only express surprise that the King's generosity did not obtain general approbation. "I should have thought," he said, "that thanks were due to the powerful monarch who, at his own sacrifice, attempted, when face to face with a great and difficult question of the day, to learn by experience the conditions necessary to the prosperity of a Productive Association, and on what rocks it most runs the risk of being wrecked with us. In this sense the King has, in a truly royal and magnanimous manner, shown munificence to the weavers of Waldenburg and other districts. . . . When the deputy was calling attention to the fact that his majesty must have had an adviser in regard to the disposition of his private benevolence, he need not have pointed to me with so many ungraceful gesticulations. I was the adviser, and I do not think I have given bad advice."

Although in the various measures which he has passed in the interest of the working classes Prince Bismarck has dived deep into the capitalist's pocket, it would not be fair to regard him as an enemy of capital. He said in the Reichstag, June 14th,

1882 : "I am not antagonistic to the rightful claims of capital ; I am far from wanting to flourish a hostile flag ; but I am of opinion that the masses, too, have rights which should be considered." On another occasion he expressly acknowledged that a land-owner had a right to proper rent, and a capitalist to proper interest, but he added that a labourer had an equal right to work. He is so far from assenting to the one-sided theories of orthodox Socialism, that he views the accumulation of wealth with favour. Opulence is a thing to be desired, and the growth of an opulent class can only be to the benefit of society.

"I wish," he once told the Reichstag, "I wish we could immediately create a few hundred millionaires. They would expend their money in the country, and this expenditure would act fruitfully on labour all round. They could not eat their money themselves ; they would have to spend the interest on it. Be glad, then, when people become rich with us. The community at large, and not only the tax authority, is sure to benefit." Political economists might tell him that views of this kind are deceptive ; their reasoning would not, however, convince him to a contrary belief.

Entertaining no antipathy against capital, it is no wonder that Prince Bismarck is no enemy either of the land-owning class. To this class he belongs himself, yet considerations higher and more weighty than mere self-interest have induced him to promote many legislative measures which he has believed to be necessary to the prosperity of the owners and cultivators of the soil. Among such measures may be named protective duties, reforms in taxation, and the laws concerning usury. As he admires the millionaire, so he admires—and even more—the great land-owner, so long as he is sensible of his duties, and not only jealous of his rights. The Chancellor remarked in the Reichstag on February 14th, 1885 :—

"The large land-owner who lives in the country is not the worst evil ; the worst is the large land-owner who lives in the town, be it Paris, Rome, or Berlin, and who only requires money from his estates and agents, who does not represent his estates in the Reichstag or Landtag, and does not even know how it fares with them. Therein lies the evil of large estates. Large estates whose owners live in the country are under certain circumstances a great blessing, and very useful ; and if England allows her large land-owners to be gradually ruined by the retention of her present corn laws, I do not believe the result will be beneficial to the future of the country or the welfare of the rural population. The large land-owners will then become *rentiers* living in town both summer and winter, knowing country life no longer, and at the most leaving town occasionally for a fine hunting expedition. I regard it as one of the greatest superiorities of our life in Germany that a large part of our well-to-do classes live all the year round, one year after another, in the country, carrying on agriculture themselves ; and when one sees the sunburnt gentlemen at five o'clock in the morning riding about their fields, and cultivating the land with the sweat of their brows, he may well say : ' May God long preserve us such land-owners who remain in the country all the year round ! ' Such as live always in the town—I am unfortunately compelled to do so, though truly I would not do it voluntarily—who lease their estates and manage them thence, and only look for remittances of money, I do not care so much about ; and I should be very willing to co-operate with Herr Bebel (a Socialist Deputy) in preventing land from accumulating in their hands. But I regard the large land-owners who are really farmers, and buy land from a predilection for this industry, as a blessing for our country, and especially for the provinces where I live. And if you succeeded in destroying this race, you would see the result in the palsying of our entire economic and political life. . . . But so long as God is still minded to preserve the German Empire and the kingdom of Prussia, this war of yours against landed proprietorship will not succeed, however many allies you may obtain."

Not less enthusiastic is Prince Bismarck in praise of the peasantry. An old German adage runs : " *Hat der Bauer Geld, hat's die ganze Welt*" ("If the peasant has money, everybody has "), and he believes a thriving peasant class to be one of the best guarantees not only of economic prosperity but of national stability.

" Peasants and large landed proprietors," he said in the

Reichstag on February 16th, 1885, "recognise more and more that they form one and the same class, the class of land-owners, and follow one and the same industry of agriculture. . . . The land-owners are, on the whole, a support of the monarchy, and their entire disposition is favourable to the existing Government; and you try to sow discord amongst them because you are displeased that the unification is proceeding gradually and unceasingly. This is the salutary effect of legislation which at first was painfully felt by many of the privileged class : the abolition of all the legal and axiomatic prerogatives of the greatest land proprietors, and especially of the earlier knighthood. We larger land-owners are in our industry to-day nothing more than the largest peasants, and the peasant is nothing more than the smaller land-owner. Indeed, most peasants call themselves land-owners, while some call themselves husbandmen and others countrymen."

Still, while naturally leaning towards the land-owning class, Prince Bismarck has never assented to the theory of absolute rights in the possession of property. On the contrary, he maintains that land-owners, like all other people, hold their property subject to the power of the State to interfere with their use and disposal of it should public interests demand such interposition. Prince Bismarck is a warm admirer of the Stein and Hardenberg land law reforms, which he has often held up as a precedent justifying State interference with private rights. Addressing the Reichstag on March 15th, 1884, he declared that when existing rights were opposed to the interests of the commonwealth, the State had a right to step in and, "cutting with the knife of the operator," to create new and healthy conditions.

His views on the question of labour and its rights are very far-going. Not only does he hold that the capitalist and landed classes are in duty bound to treat liberally the labour upon which both are so greatly dependent, but that the State owes peculiar obligations to the working classes by reason of their general inability to protect themselves against the excessive power and influence of property. In 1884, when speaking upon the industrial insurance question, he went so far as to proclaim the doctrine of a "right to work." "Give the working-man the right to work as long as he is healthy," he said on May 9th ; "assure him care when he is sick ; assure him maintenance when he is old. If you do that, and do not fear the sacrifice, or cry out at State Socialism directly the words ' provision for old age ' are uttered,—if the State will show a little more Christian solicitude for the working-man, then I believe that the gentlemen of the Wyden (Social-Democratic) programme will sound their bird-call in vain, and that the thronging to them will cease as soon as working-men see that the Government and legislative bodies are earnestly concerned for their welfare."

To the sneer of an opponent he added : " Yes, I acknowledge unconditionally a right to work, and I will stand up for it as long as I am in this place. But here I do not stand upon the ground of Socialism, which is said to have only begun with the Bismarck Ministry, but on that of the Prussian common law.[1] . . . Was not the right to work openly proclaimed at the time of the publication of the common law ? Is it not established in all our social arrangements that the man who comes before his fellow-citizens and says, ' I am healthy, I desire to work, but can find no work,' is entitled to say also, ' Give me work,' and that the State is bound to give him work ?" [2] " But large public works would be necessary," objected his opponents. " Of course," was Bismarck's rejoinder ; " let them be undertaken : Why not ? It is the State's duty." [3] As yet, however, Prince Bismarck has made no attempt to give practical effect to this theory.

---

[1] See page 19.

[2] At a Parliamentary *Soirée* given the same day in the Chancellor's palace the question gave rise to considerable debate. According to a report in the semi-official *North German Gazette*, Bismarck defended his thesis to the utmost. " I still hold to the right to work as I advanced it in the Reichstag," he said. " Prussian common law contains here as often elsewhere excellent provisions. I must say, too, that I do not regard the consequences of this right as so very serious or so far-going. Already no one is with us allowed to hunger. If relief is primarily only given to those incapable of working—if some one says that he can work, and wishes to work, yet can find no work, we cannot simply leave him to himself, and we do not do so. That would induce despair. If we were to execute useful works at the public cost it would be quite justifiable. We should thus be merely giving to the workman, instead of public alms, more abundant and worthier assistance."

[3] When the German Parliament was being constituted at Frankfort in 1848, the demand of a " right to work " as well as protection for labour was made both within and without that assembly. A congress of artisans and workpeople

held at Berlin required the State to guarantee work to every one who wished for work, the labour being suited to his powers, and the wages adequate to his needs. The democratic party in the Parliament brought forward proposals for securing work for the unemployed, to be provided by the parish or the State, but they were rejected. During the Berlin revolution of 1848 the municipal authorities afforded work to a large number of unemployed by undertaking constructive works on a great scale. Want of work had very much to do with the violence of the mobs which kept Berlin in terror at that time. One day a crowd of some thousands of labourers went to the Labour Minister's residence and demanded work. When the Minister offered them money they turned on him with the angry cry : " We are not beggars ; we are free working-men ; we do not want alms, but work." Nor would they accept the offered gift.

CHAPTER IV.

THE NEW EMPIRE.

PRINCE BISMARCK'S economic legislation owed its origin to two causes. The first of these causes was the unprosperous condition into which German trade, industry, and agriculture had fallen during the first years following the re-establishment of the Empire. This decline had not, indeed, been sudden. It had been going on for many years, but the remarkable quickening of national life caused by the brilliant military achievements of 1870 and their political results had offered a check whose influence continued effectual for some years. This influence, however, becoming exhausted, the downward movement was resumed ; and when the Chancellor in 1879 proposed to remodel Germany's economic system, national prosperity was at a very low ebb. The second cause was purely social, and it was twofold : viz., the unhappy position of the working classes and the threatening growth of Socialism. It will be necessary to consider these causes in detail.

Already we have seen that early in the sixties Free Trade theories began to gain the upper hand in Prussian official circles. The French Government had lately taken important steps in the same direction, while England had gone over to Free Trade nearly twenty years before. A good deal of the credit for Prussia's gradual conversion to what soon began to be known as " Manchesterdom " (" *Manchesterthum* "), is due to the Economic Congress established at Gotha in 1858. This congress was made up of members representative of all German States. At its gatherings proposals favourable to the spread of Free Trade principles were discussed, and resolutions were passed. But the influence of the congress was not confined to academic debates. It was regarded as the duty of the delegates to take measures to popularise the principles and aims of the congress in their individual States, and many of them discharged this obligation to good effect. The congress represented essentially the interests of trade, shipping, and capital, but not the interests of agriculture and the land. Nevertheless Prussia's economic legislation was largely informed by the spirit of this assembly until the middle of the seventies. We know on Prince Bismarck's own authority that he was never in sympathy with Free Trade so far as concerns Germany. He has, indeed, declared that he "holds Free Trade to be altogether false," as an absolute principle. But during the period of Liberal ascendency in economic affairs his attention was wholly occupied with the weightier matters of State, and he acquiesced in what was done without taking the trouble to inquire whether it was right or wrong. He was surrounded by ministers imbued with Liberal principles, and it was due to their influence that Prussia and afterwards the new Empire embarked on a policy nearly akin to that of Free Trade, a policy which continued uninterrupted until 1878 or 1879.

But the Free Traders were not to be allowed to retain predominance for ever. A reaction had for some years been increasing in strength, and it was soon to make its influence felt in practical ways. Just as in 1858 the trading and monied interests established an organisation for the spread of Manchester principles, so the agrarian party and the advocates of protection formed an association with the purpose of convincing the Government and the nation of the necessity for returning to the old Prussian policy. This association, the Association for Social Politics (*Verein für Sozialpolitik*), was established at Eisenach in 1872 ; and though it partook somewhat of an academic character, its influence upon the social-political laws of the last fifteen years has been considerable. Its ruling idea was the untenableness in modern times of the *Laissez-faire* principle, the one-sidedness of the theory that the State should restrict its activity to the mere maintenance of the law and the promotion of peace without and within. It demanded State encouragement and protection of trade, industry, and agriculture, State promotion of the interests of culture in general, and State intervention for the improvement of the working-man's condition.

Various circumstances tended to favour the propaganda of the Eisenach school, and especially the commercial and financial crisis which followed the famous Bubble Era in 1873. The French war, with its political consequences, gave a mighty impulse to German national life. It heralded a new birth. Old things passed away and all things became new. What the French humiliation did for Germany in a political sense, the French indemnity did for her commercially. The dispersal of the milliards filled the country with gold, and the phenomenal condition of the money market led to a perfect mania of speculation. A wild race after fortune was run, and all classes entered the competition. Nobleman and manufacturer, Government official and petty pensioner, Jew and Greek, shopkeeper and artisan were alike inflamed by the suicidal passion for gold. The entire economic condition of the country became changed. Production increased to an enormous extent. Speculation on the Stock Exchange and elsewhere took dimensions and forms never heard of before or since. Those who had money squandered it with a prodigal hand, and those who had it not gambled with borrowed gold and with doubtful credit. For a time all went well. It might have seemed that a commercial millennium had arrived. Many fortunes were made. Industries which had hitherto languished showed the appearance of prosperity. Wages rose, and for a time the working classes seemed to have been placed upon a new and higher level of existence. But the beautiful picture was soon found to have a sad reverse. The inevitable reaction set in. The French milliards became exhausted; enterprise slackened; and the revival of mercantile prosperity proved a delusion and a snare. The credit market was entirely disorganised. A host of undertakings launched by unscrupulous adventurers, and floated by the money of inexperienced Peter Simples, turned out to be as rotten as touchwood. Many other enterprises, introduced to the world amid the trumpeting of highly respectable but too sanguine promoters, shared similar disaster; and when the aggregate balance-sheet of the bubble companies was drawn up, it was seen that while a vast amount of capital had been frittered away, the only people who had benefited were the wire-pullers, whom abundance of wit and resource compensated for want of conscience.[1] Trade and industry had the same tale of misfortune to tell. Manufacturers woke up one morning to find the market glutted past hope of recovery. Goods had been produced in quantities which the demand did not justify, and it was impossible to find buyers either at home or abroad. Failure followed failure. Factories were stopped, warehouses were closed, and industrial fortunes, built up slowly by the accumulation of hard-earned profits, disappeared like the snow beneath the sun. Labour fared even worse than capital. The wages which had risen so rapidly fell with a shock, where, through the cessation of employment, they were not entirely lost to the toiler's family.

Agriculture, too, had long been suffering severely. Prices had fallen while taxation had risen. In many parts corn could no longer be grown at a profit on account of the enormous imports of foreign grain, and the area under cultivation had considerably decreased. The imports of rye, barley, and oats over the Russo-Prussian frontier or by the Baltic Sea had doubled in two years :—

	Rye.	Barley.	Oats.
1875	6,869,324	530,107	2,368,663 cwts.
1876	11,361,144	594,312	3,196,049 ,,
1877	13,266,203	1,920,778	3,620,447 ,,

The imports of American corn had also increased greatly.

The disastrous commercial crisis which Germany passed through at this time gave great stimulus to the movement for protection. The reactionary party redoubled its efforts, and by means of the Parliamentary tribune, the public platform, the Press, and by pamphlets and ephemeral literature endeavoured to convince the country of the folly of " Manchesterdom."

But success was not to be attained just yet. Prince Bismarck has placed it on record that the year 1877 was the decisive year in which he came to a turning-point in his life so far as concerned economical and social questions. Then he began to make economics a serious study. He has said :—

" During the first fifteen years of my ministerial activity I was absorbed by foreign politics, and I did not feel called upon to

---

[1] See Appendix B : " The Bubble Era."

trouble myself much with the internal politics of the Empire, nor had I the requisite time. I took it for granted that the internal affairs were in good hands. Afterwards, when I lost the help which I had thought reliable, I was compelled to look into matters myself, and I found that though I had up to then sworn *in verba magistri*, the actual results did not come up to the expectations which underlay our legislation. I had the impression that since the introduction of the Free Trade system in 1865 we fell into atrophy, which was only checked for a time by the new blood of the five milliard contribution, and that it was necessary to adopt a remedy."

Up to 1876 Bismarck had entrusted the country's economic policy entirely to Minister von Delbrück, but in that year this colleague resigned office. The reason given for the withdrawal of Dr. Delbrück was "motives of health," but every one knew that he left the Chancellor because of irreconcilable disagreement of views. The resignation of Dr. Delbrück, who occupied the position of President of the Chancellery, was followed by that of Herr Camphausen, Minister of Finance, and before two years had passed the Ministers of Commerce and the Interior had also withdrawn from office. Everything was now propitious for the inauguration of a new economic era. Prince Bismarck referred as follows in the Prussian Lower House on February 4th, 1881, to the Delbrück secession :—

"Before I concerned myself personally with customs questions, I did not represent my own convictions, but those of my colleague Delbrück, whom I regarded as the right man in the right place, for I had no time to form my own views. . . . It was the retirement of Delbrück which compelled me to form views for myself and to express them. I cannot properly say that I formerly held other views than now : you might as well dispute with me as to whether I had been of this or that opinion, had held this or that theory, respecting some scientific question. I had no time to form a definite picture of mercantile politics. I deny that my former views were opposed to my present, for I had none : I was the obedient disciple of Herr Delbrück, and I expressed his views when I expressed views at all. But when he retired from the partnership, I was compelled to represent my own opinions, which perhaps deviated in many respects from his; but I certainly did not formerly hold contrary opinions, which now I have changed."

The other side of Prince Bismarck's new policy was in the narrower sense of the word social. Here he was primarily influenced by the discontent of the working classes, which had found loud and emphatic expression in the phenomenal growth of Socialism. That discontent was due to various causes, some political, some economical and industrial. German Socialism is unlike the Socialism of other countries in that it sprang from a political soil. Social factors in time exercised great influence upon its growth and form, but the seed and soil were alike political. The first perceptible impulse came from the French Revolution of last century, but the national decline of the German States, and of the absolute government which was one of their oldest traditions, effectually prevented any response to the lawless cries which were wafted across the Rhine in 1789. During the next half-century, however, the political aspirations of the German peoples grew in vigour, and the revolutionary movements of both 1830 and 1848 produced great excitement amongst not a few of the heterogeneous populations, and greater still amongst the various Governments.

It was in the latter year that Germany formally opened her doors to Socialism.[1] Hitherto the forces of Communism, Socialism, and revolution had united for the subversion of the existing political system. With the granting of constitutions to many of the States, political agitation declined, and Socialistic agitation took clear and definite form. "Socialism emerged from the convulsions and the ferment of those years as a fresh goal of popular aspirations. It was Socialism that remained after the earthquake, the tempest, and the fire had passed away. Succeeding events greatly stimulated the new movement. Politically the working-man became free, for the equality of all citizens in the eyes of the law passed from the region of theory to that of fact.

---

[1] "German Socialism and Ferdinand Lassalle" (by the same author), p. 22. To this work the reader is referred for an extended consideration of early as well as modern Socialistic movements in Germany.

The development of industry, however, exerted quite a contrary effect, for it perpetuated and increased the economic and social subjection of the labouring classes. The more the capitalist system was extended, the more social inequalities multiplied. The law made equal and capitalism made unequal. Thus the position of the labourer became ambiguous. As a citizen and a subject of the State he was perfectly free, sharing the civil rights of the wealthiest; but as a member of the community of industry he occupied a position in reality dependent and unfree. It was inevitable that this condition of things should conduce to social discontent and class antagonism." [1]

In the middle of the century wages were everywhere very low, and the standard of life amongst the working classes was in consequence the same. Statistics of the period show that as a result of arduous toil, long hours, and poor food, the mortality amongst working-men was far higher in Prussia than in England or France. The social and economic inequalities which made the lot of the labourer so unhappy told greatly in favour of Socialism, which had at the time powerful advocates in the persons of men like Marx and Lassalle. Schulze-Delitzsch tried to induce the working classes to seek salvation in the co-operative movement, and he was successful in establishing numerous societies between the years 1849 and 1858, when his cause reached its high-water mark. This movement, however, never touched the poorer of the working classes. Those who chiefly and almost exclusively benefited by it were artisans and people possessing small capitals. As an antidote against Socialism co-operation failed. Possibly Schulze-Delitzsch might have been more successful had not a rival appeared upon the scene in Ferdinand Lassalle, the father of German Social-Democracy, whose brief public career did more for the Socialistic cause than the previous half-century of indiscriminate agitation. On Lassalle's death in 1864 there was a series of inglorious contests amongst the more prominent of his followers for the vacant leadership of the party he had organised and led to triumph, but in spite of dissensions the cause continued to grow rapidly.

---

[1] "German Socialism and Ferdinand Lassalle," pp. 33, 34.

In 1871 the Socialists returned two members to the Reichstag, three years later their representation increased to nine, and in 1877 the number of Socialist deputies was twelve. The Socialist votes polled in the first ordinary returns were : in 1871, 124,665, out of a total of 3,892,160; 1874, 351,952, out of 5,190,254; and 1877, 493,288, out of 5,401,021. In the last year the political parties represented in the Reichstag numbered fourteen, and the Socialist party took the eighth place in point of Parliamentary representatives and the fifth in point of votes polled. Up to the year 1878 Prince Bismarck had planned no measure of repression against the Socialists, though he had long been suspicious of their growing strength. In that year, however, two attempts—the first on May 11th and the second on June 2nd—were made upon the life of the aged Emperor William, and the universal horror and anger created by the crimes enabled the Chancellor to carry on October 19th, 1878, a drastic law intended to check Socialistic agitation. Prince Bismarck had on his side the combined forces of Conservatism in passing this law through the Reichstag, and both he and his supporters believed that the object aimed at would be attained.

The predictions of the Progressist leader, Herr Richter, have, however, been abundantly verified. " I fear Social-Democracy more under this law than without it," he said two days before the measure was promulgated, having been voted in the final division by 221 members against 149. A striking commentary upon these words is offered by the returns of Parliamentary elections. While in 1877 the Socialist vote was 493,288, it was 763,128, or over ten per cent. of all votes cast, in 1885; and in 1890 the Socialists polled more than a million votes.

While passing repressive legislation, Prince Bismarck let it be understood that he intended it to go hand in hand with important social reforms. With one hand he would use the rod, and with the other apply assuasive means. He refused to believe that the working classes of Germany had committed themselves past recall to the theories of Socialism. He maintained rather that those who followed the lead of men like Bebel and Liebknecht were people of the "baser sort," and that the honourable and industrious sections of the army of labour still respected the law and had no wish to disturb the existing social system. His aim in promoting industrial reforms was to cut the ground beneath the Socialistic agitators by gradually removing those grievances of which they could with only too much justice complain. He told the Reichstag on October 9th, 1878 :—

"I will further every endeavour which positively aims at improving the condition of the working classes. . . . As soon as a positive proposal came from the Socialists for fashioning the future in a sensible way, in order that the lot of the working-man might be improved, I would not at any rate refuse to examine it favourably, and I would not even shrink from the idea of State help for the people who would help themselves."

The outcome of this and other declarations to the same effect was the promise, in the imperial speech with which the Reichstag was opened in February, 1879, of social reforms for the amelioration of the condition of the working classes. This promise was repeated several times during the next two years ; and finally it was on February 15th, 1881, definitely announced, in an imperial message, that laws for the insurance of workpeople would without delay be laid before the Reichstag.

Here, in brief, are the causes which led to Prince Bismarck's policy of State Socialism. They were on the one hand economic, and on the other social. At a time when trade, industry, and agriculture were alike bordering on ruin, and when society was being undermined by the misery and discontent of the working classes, all eyes turned to the State for succour. Self-help stood paralysed, unable to grapple with the terrible difficulties of the situation. After long wandering in the wilderness of Individualism, which had led only to misfortune and unhappiness, people besought the State to extricate them from their sad straits. They sighed for the flesh-pots of Egypt. The time had now come when Germany was to return to the economic and social policy of old Prussia, and the question of customs duties was taken in hand first. It was in 1877 that the Chancellor resolved in his own mind that a change in the economic system of the country was necessary ; and directly he saw that the sense of the nation was with him, the resolution to act promptly was taken.

> " Im Anfang war das Wort,   .   .   .
> Im Anfang war der Sinn,   .   .   .
> Im Anfang war die Kraft,   .   .   .
> Im Anfang war *die That*."

Before the Liberals had had time to recover from the shock occasioned by the announcement of Prince Bismarck's altered views, measures were laid before the Reichstag which were to revolutionise Germany's economic policy.

CHAPTER V.

BEFORE the time reached protectionist tendencies had occasionally been betrayed by isolated members of the Reichstag, but
a reactionary policy had not hitherto been advocated or favoured
by a strong Parliamentary party. During a debate on December
7th, 1875, on the prevailing crisis in the iron trade, the demand
was made that the duties abolished by the law of July 7th,
1873—which was to take place in 1877—should be maintained.
The Government, however, through Minister von Delbrück,
refused to interfere, and the matter was not again heard of. In
the spring of 1877, too, the Chancellor was asked to institute
an inquiry into the condition of trade and agriculture, but nothing
of the kind was done at the time. It was not long, however,
before the Government was compelled to move. No fewer than
two hundred and four members of the Conservative, National
Liberal, and Catholic parties entered the " Free Economic Union
of the Reichstag," with a view to investigate the question of
economic and fiscal reform, and in October, 1878, they published
a declaration calling for a revision of the customs tariff, in view
of the hostile mercantile policies pursued by neighbouring States
and the severe depression then afflicting trade and agriculture.
The declaration was published on October 17th, and a week
later the Government was interpellated on the question. The
Chancellor replied that the Federal Governments had so far
come to no decision, but he was himself favourable to the appeal
of the Economic Union, and he promised that no further commercial treaties should be concluded until the country's entire
economic system had been examined.

It is not clear that the Government at this time contemplated
the introduction of strictly protective duties. In the previous
August the Finance Ministers of the various German States had

met at Heidelberg to consider the financial condition of the Empire, and had drawn up a scheme for the augmentation of the imperial revenues by a series of fiscal duties. Now, however, that Prince Bismarck saw how the wind was blowing, he determined to widen the scope of the reforms proposed. The programme of the Heidelberg conference was laid on one side, and the Chancellor asked the Federal Council to appoint a committee to consider the revision of the whole tariff. This proposal was accepted, and before the end of the year a committee of fifteen members had been nominated. On December 15th, 1878, the Chancellor addressed to the committee a memorable letter, in which for the first time he developed a scheme of taxation and protection. After premising that financial reform was his first consideration, and that he sought to increase the Empire's revenues by means of indirect rather than direct taxation, he expressed his conviction of the desirability of returning to the principle of the "customs liability of all imported articles," which "was laid down in the Prussian customs legislation from the year 1818 onward, and later found expression in the universal import duty imposed by the customs tariff of the *Zollverein* up to 1865. Exemption from this liability to pay duty would be allowed to raw materials indispensable to industry which, like cotton, cannot be produced in Germany, and, according to circumstances, to those which can only be produced in insufficient quantity or quality. All articles not specially exempted should be subjected to an import duty graduated according to the value of the commodity and on the basis of various percentages, according to the requirements of home production. The customs rates thus to be laid down would be reduced to weight-units, as is the rule in the existing customs tariff, and in this way levied, so far as from the nature of the object the levy of the duty may not be desirable per piece (as in the case of cattle) or according to value (as in the case of railway carriages or iron river craft)."

The imports of the year 1877 amounted to 3,877,000,000 marks, and articles to the declared value of 2,853,000,000 marks were admitted free of duty. Prince Bismarck estimated that under the new system articles would be exempted of duty to the value of 1,400,000,000 marks, and that if the future import duty averaged 5 per cent. *ad valorem*, the revenue from customs would yield an additional 70,000,000 marks yearly to the imperial treasury. But the financial argument was not the only one that commended the revision of the tariff. There was the economic and mercantile aspect of the question.

" I leave undecided," proceeded the letter, "the question whether complete mutual freedom of international commerce, such as is contemplated by the theory of free trade, would not serve the interests of Germany. But as long as most of the countries with which our trade is carried on surround themselves with customs barriers, which there is still a growing tendency to multiply, it does not seem to me justifiable, or to the economic interest of the nation, that we should allow ourselves to be restricted in the satisfaction of our financial wants by the apprehension that German products will thereby be but slightly preferred to foreign ones. The existing *Verein* tariff contains, together with the purely fiscal duties, a series of moderate protective duties intended to benefit certain branches of industry. The abolition or decrease of these duties does not appear advisable, especially in the present position of industry. Perhaps, indeed, it would be well to reintroduce duties on a number of articles, or to increase the present rates, in the interest of various depressed branches of home industry, in accordance with the results of the commissions now in progress. Yet protective duties for individual industries, when they exceed the limit imposed by regard for their financial proceeds, act as a privilege and arouse on the part of representatives of unprotected industries the antipathy to which every privilege is exposed. A customs system which secures to the entire home production a preference before foreign production in the home market, while keeping within the limits imposed by financial interests, will not run the risk of this antipathy. Such a system will in no way appear partial, because its effects will be more equally spread over all the productive circles of the land than is the case with a system of protective duties for isolated branches of industry. The minority of the population, which does not produce at all but exclusively consumes, will apparently be injured by a customs system favouring the entire national production. Yet if by means of such a system the aggregate sum of the values produced in the country increase, and thus the national wealth be on the whole enhanced, the non-producing parts of the population—and especially the State and communal officials who are dependent upon a fixed money income—will eventually be benefited; for means of counterbalancing hardships will be at the command of the community in case the extension of customs-liability to the entire imports should result in an increase of the prices of the necessaries of life. Yet with low duties such an increase will in all probability not take place to the extent to which consumers are accustomed to apprehend, just as, on the other hand, the prices of bread and meat have not fallen to an appreciable degree in consequence of the abolition of the duties on corn-grinding and cattle-killing in the parishes where these used to exist. The real financial duties, imposed on articles which are not produced at home and the import of which is indispensable, will in part fall upon the consumer alone. On the contrary, with articles which the country is able to produce in quantity and quality adequate to the home consumption, the foreign producer will alone have to bear the duty in order that he may compete in the German market. Finally, in cases in which part of the home demand must be covered by foreign supply, the foreign producer will in general be compelled to bear at least a part and often the whole of the duty, and thus to reduce his profit to the extent of this amount."

Upon these lines the revision of the customs tariff was to be conducted. The financial necessities of the Empire were to be provided for, but at the same time industry, trade, and agriculture were to be afforded protection against foreign competition. The Chancellor's declaration was followed by a forecast of legislation, contained in a speech from the throne dated February 12th, 1879. In this the Emperor stated:—

"The Federal Governments are considering legislative measures for the removal, or at least the diminution, of the economic evils from which we are suffering. The proposals which I have made, and still intend to make, to my allies aim, by providing the Empire with new sources of revenue, at placing the Governments in a position to desist from levying the taxes which they and

their Legislatures recognise as the hardest to enforce. At the same
time I am of opinion that the country's entire economic activity
has a right to claim all the support which legislative adjustment
of duties and taxes can afford, and which in the lands with which
we trade is, perhaps, afforded beyond actual requirement. I
regard it as my duty to adopt measures to preserve the German
market to national production so far as is consistent with the
general interest; and our customs legislation must accordingly
revert to the tried principles upon which the prosperous career of
the *Zollverein* rested for nearly half a century, but which have in
important particulars been deserted in our mercantile policy since
1865. I cannot admit that actual success has attended this
change in our customs policy."

A few days later, February 21st, Prince Bismarck gave open expression to protectionist views. "I propose," he said, "to return
to the time-honoured ways of 1823 to 1865. We left them in
the latter year." He declared frankly that though self-contradic-
tion did not tend to increase one's dignity, he was willing to confess his past error, for the interests of the country required it. It
was necessary that the fiscal policy should be changed, and he
was ready to change it himself or to make way for somebody
else likewise prepared to undertake the duty. Deputy Richter
charged him with having had secret protectionist sympathies in
1862, when he became Prussian Minister President, but the
Chancellor denied the imputation, while not shrinking from it.
"I should be proud if, as is alleged, I had had 'economic tendencies' of any kind in 1862; but I must confess, to my shame,
that I had none at all." Those days, however, brought him
other and weightier duties than the direction of Prussia's economic
policy. He had then to do with grave imperial questions, with
constitutional and diplomatic problems of far-reaching consequences, with military enterprises which would either make or
mar his country. "I did not," he said, "mix myself up with
economical questions, but endeavoured to secure the most prominent statesmen who were willing to assist in carrying out the
work which I had undertaken. Undoubtedly I did not entertain
the economic views of Herr Delbrück, and though we were not
agreed, I do not know how the various questions between us were

settled; but I suppose I must have surrendered in most cases, for I willingly made sacrifices, both politically and in my own opinions, in order to retain an uncommonly effective co-operation for the cause to which I was devoted."

The revised customs tariff came before the Reichstag for first consideration on May 2nd. It was accompanied by a voluminous *Begründung*—a statement setting forth the reasons for legislation —in which the Government maintained that only by stringent measures of protection could the national market be preserved for native industry and agriculture. The iron trade was said to be languishing, and "iron producers as a whole regard the re-introduction and partial increase of the iron duties as the only remedy. The representatives of the industries engaged in the manufacture of machinery, tools, and other implements likewise call for protection." As to corn, it was stated that the market was flooded with foreign produce, sold at rates with which home producers could not compete, so that ruin stared them in the face. "It is, therefore, not only to the interest of the farmers, but to that of the entire community, that corn-growing should be maintained."

Prince Bismarck opened the debate by explaining the fiscal side of the Government's scheme. But a larger revenue was not all that was wanted. Industry must unconditionally be protected. Hitherto Germany, owing to the policy of practical Free Trade, had been a country where the goods of all the world might be deposited, the result being to depress home prices and to destroy home trade. "Let us close our doors and erect somewhat higher barriers," said the Chancellor, "and let us thus take care to preserve at least the German market to German industry. The chances of a large export trade are nowadays exceedingly precarious. There are now no more great countries to discover. The globe is circumnavigated, and we can no longer find any large purchasing nations. Commercial treaties, it is true, are under certain circumstances favourable to foreign trade; but whenever a treaty is concluded, it is a question of *Qui trompe-t-on ici?*—who is taken in? As a rule one of the parties is, but only after a number of years is it known which one." He declared that in remodelling the economic system of the country national interests would alone be considered.

In defending the proposed increase of the corn duties the Chancellor had to oppose Dr. Delbrück's contention that the only result would be to make the price of grain dearer without benefiting agriculture. He laid down the proposition that low corn prices are an economic evil. The position of the farmer depends upon the revenue he obtains from the sale of his produce, and the better his position the more prosperous is the nation's economic life as a whole.

"If cheap corn is the goal at which we should aim, we ought long ago to have abolished the land tax, for it burdens the industry which produces corn at home, which produces 400 million cwts. against the 27 or 30 millions which we import. But no one has ever dreamed of such a thing; on the contrary, in times when theory has been the same as now, the land tax has been gradually increased throughout Germany so far as I know, and in Prussia 30 per cent. since 1861, being increased from 30 to 40 million marks."

He held that farmers had a right to demand that the home market should be saved to them. Prices were so depressed that it was already a question whether agriculture could be carried on successfully. If the time should come when corn could not be profitably cultivated, "not only agriculture, but the Prussian State, and the German Empire itself, would go to ruin." This eventuality would not, however, occur. "Twenty million German farmers will not allow themselves to be ruined. It is only necessary that they should become conscious of what is before them, and they will try to defend themselves by legal and constitutional means."

The Radical party opposed the Government's reactionary policy to the last, but the country was on the side of the proposed change, and the revised tariff passed into law on July 7th, 1879, when, by saying good-bye to Free Trade, Germany ceased, according to the Chancellor's view, to be "the dupe of an honest conviction." The voting was: for the new tariff, 217; against, 117. The Conservative party, the Clericals, sixteen members of the National Liberal party, and the Alsace-Lorraine members voted for the tariff; and the Radicals, the majority of the National Liberals, and the Social-Democrats opposed it.

It would be a mistake to suppose that Prince Bismarck is in favour of unconditional protection. With him Free Trade and Protection are categories of time and place. He regards neither principle as apodictically true. What is good for one country may be very bad for another. It is, in fact, a question of expediency, not of natural law. He has pointed out that England herself, the home of Free Trade, "used to have high protective duties until the time came when she had been so strengthened under protection that she could come forward as a Herculean combatant, and challenge all the world with 'Enter the lists against me!'" As England was led by self-interest to Free Trade, Germany was led by self-interest to Protection. In this as in all matters Prince Bismarck refuses to be guided by the dicta of science. "In the domain of political economy," he once said, "the abstract doctrines of science leave me perfectly cold, my only standard of judgment being experience." It is not hard to understand how a statesman of his strong national sympathies should, in view of the prevailing industrial and agricultural decline, have resorted to so extreme a measure as the reversal of the country's economic policy.

It now remains to glance at the later modifications of the policy adopted in 1879. Two years later Prince Bismarck felt so confident of the success of his bold enterprise that he declared to the Reichstag (March 28th, 1881) : "In the development of our tariff I am determined to oppose any modification in the direction of Free Trade, and to use my influence in favour of greater protection and of a higher revenue from frontier duties." Three years later (December 1st, 1884) he could tell Parliament that the new commercial policy had " freed the country from its poverty of blood," and that the prosperity of trade and industry generally was on the increase. Home and foreign commerce was larger, and there was greater briskness in the shipping of all or most of the ports. Agriculture alone had failed to benefit by the increased duties. Industry had evidently reaped good results from the outset, for the exports of manufactures had grown from 1,026,500,000 marks in 1878 to 1,368,300,000 marks in 1880, an increase of 341,800,000 millions, or over 33 per cent., in three years. Better still, wages were, even by 1880, higher in many trades, even though the prices of a large number of manufactures had fallen. By the year 1885 further advance still had been made. Taking 103 large industrial companies, it could be shown that, while in 1878–79 the percentage of profits was only 2·29 per cent., it was 5·30 per cent. in 1884–85. Again, 206 large smelting and machine works employed in 1885 40·5 per cent. more men than in 1879, and their wages had substantially increased. Of these works 89 were companies; and while in 1879 only 55 worked at profit, the number which so worked in 1884 was 79. A comprehensive return prepared by the Association of German Iron and Steel Manufacturers, embracing 247 works, showed that the number of employees was in 1884 over 35 per cent. more than in 1879. This greater trade had an appreciable effect upon shipping. While the tonnage of German steam and sailing ships was 1,117,935 the year before the passing of the new tariff, it was 1,294,288 in 1885. The number of sailing vessels had greatly decreased, in consequence of the growing competition of steam; but the increase in the number of sea-going steamships had been so marked—from 336, with a tonnage of 183,379, in 1878, to 650, with a tonnage of 413,943, in 1885—that the falling off was more than compensated for. While, again, only 21,472 German vessels, with a tonnage of 2,505,779, arrived in home ports in 1875, the number in 1885 was 36,115, and the tonnage 4,513,692. On the other hand, 18,223 German vessels, with a tonnage of 2,076,234, left home ports in 1875, and 34,211, with a tonnage of 3,989,052, in 1885. It is one of Prince Bismarck's favourite theories that increasing emigration is a sign of prosperity. His argument is as follows :—The emigrant requires capital to enable him to leave his country, if not to settle in his new home. This capital is the result of saving. A small emigration indicates that the home-weary people who are financially equipped for the costly undertaking of leaving one country for another are few in number. According to the Chancellor's theory of emigration, the years succeeding the introduction of the new tariff must have been prosperous ones; for while in 1879 the emigrants by way of German ports and Antwerp numbered 33,327, the number was 106,190 in 1880 and 210,547 in 1881, though it fell to 143,586 in 1884.

However trade may have benefited by the measure of 1879, it is certain that agriculture did not improve. Prince Bismarck had, during the discussion of the new tariff, expressed the conviction that the price of food would not be increased. This prediction proved correct, for, instead of rising, prices fell considerably, owing largely to foreign competition, which, though it received a temporary check, continued to press heavily on the home corn-growers. To take Prussia alone, while the average price of wheat per 100 kilog. was 22·7 marks during the twelve years 1867 to 1878, and 21·1 marks during the years 1879 to 1882, it fell to 18·5 marks in 1883 and to 17·3 in 1884. The prices of rye for the same periods were 17·7, 17·5, 14·7, and 14·7 marks respectively ; of barley, 16·5, 15·9, 14·6, and 14·9 marks ; and of oats, 15·9, 14·7, 13·7, and 14·4 marks. It was evident to the agrarian party, and it soon became evident to Prince Bismarck, that the corn duties needed raising. This work was taken in hand in 1885. The *Begründung* to the new tariff law stated that while the pro-tective measure of 1879 had " in general been attended by bene-ficial results," and had " diverted Germany's economic policy from a false course," the " natural development and amendment of the tariff " were desirable to the attainment of the purposes advocated in 1879. It was shown by statistics that the foreign producer still had his own way in the German market. The imports of wheat had fallen 50 per cent. from 1878 to 1884, but those of rye had hardly decreased at all, those of barley were unaltered, while of oats and maize a far larger quantity was imported than before the tariff was revised. The Government proposed to increase the duties on all kinds of corn, on timber, live stock, as well as a few classes of textile goods, and a few miscellaneous articles, and the Reichstag again gave a ready ear to the voice of the protector. Before this various of the States had through their legislatures declared for higher agricultural duties, and the proposal was in sympathy with the general feeling of the country. Prince Bis-marck took a prominent part in the debates. He was able to throw into the teeth of the Cassandras of 1879 all the forebodings with which they had endeavoured to prevent the first revision of the tariff.

"The fear has been expressed," he said on February 10th,

1885, "that the price of corn will, in consequence of the higher duties, increase very considerably, and that social dangers will thus arise. Well, you will remember that six years ago the same prophecies were made in this very hall, and in part by the men who have spoken to-day or who will yet speak. We were told that prices would reach such a height that they would curtail the labourer's earnings and food, and that we were inviting the social dangers which we desired to resist and remove. All these prophecies have proved false ; not one of them has been fulfilled. The corn laws of that time have everywhere worked beneficently. Only in one direction have they proved ineffective where the reverse was perhaps expected, though not by me, for I thought otherwise : they have not had the effect of improving the prices of agricultural products. On the contrary, corn is now cheaper than it has been for a long time, and in proportion to the present value of money cheaper than it has ever been this century. The effect then predicted has in no way been produced. Whether it will be produced when the duty is trebled I will not venture to say with certainty, though I hardly think it probable. It may, however, be the case, and if it is, well and good, for the farmer will benefit by an increase in prices ; but if not, the duties will certainly be borne by foreign countries ; and why should not the Finance Minister of the German Empire accept the duties which America and Russia are willing to pay him? . . . In any case I should rejoice if the law led to an increase of prices ; for the improvement of the position of the farmers would be to the advantage of the entire population, and would be far from injuring others."

He believed that Germany could produce herself all the corn she needed if only her agriculture were protected against countries more favourably situated as to climate, soil, and wages. Far more corn would be grown than in the past so soon as corn-growing became remunerative. His desire that corn prices might increase was again expressed in the following words :—

"I hope that the price of corn may increase ; I hold its increase to be necessary. There must be a limit when the State must try to raise the price of corn. I asked you to imagine the price of rye falling 50 Pfennig ; or I will name the price which now and again really occurs in the inner Russian governments, the price of one mark. Is it not quite clear that our agriculture would then be absolutely ruined—that it would not be able to exist any longer—and with it all the labourers and all the capitalists dependent upon it? Quite apart from the farmer—who is, of course, a *corpus vile* on which the town folk can experiment—though it must be remembered that the towns would no longer have buyers in the farmers; the labourers would be without employment and would stream to the towns. In short, it is undoubtedly a national calamity when the price of corn, the everyday means of subsistence, falls below the rate at which it can be cultivated with us. I will regard the maxim as admitted, that there is a limit below which the price of corn cannot fall without the ruin of our entire economic life. The question, then, is: Has this limit been reached or not? Minister Lucius has given us statistics which must compel us to admit that it has already been reached. But it should not be reached; for when it is reached it will be too late, and we shall already have suffered most enormous losses. . . . When rye with us falls to a price at which it cannot be cultivated, we are living in unsound conditions and are going to decay. This decay may be deferred by the use of the capital we may have laid up, but we create an untenable situation: this is as clear as that two and two make four."

Similarly the timber duties were intended to protect forestry in a vulnerable part. They were aimed principally at Austria and Sweden. In Silesia the forest workmen looked with mournful faces as heavy trains laden with Galician timber passed by rail through the forest. So keen was foreign competition that forestry was fast becoming an unremunerative industry. By the new duties it was hoped to keep sawn wood out of the country and to compel exporters to send timber in a raw state. Prince Bismarck said on February 10th, 1885 :—

" We wish that Swedish planks may no longer come to us, but only Swedish timber for the support of the wood industries on the Baltic coast, in Holstein, and on the North Sea coast, and as much of that as possible—more than hitherto. We only desire to ensure to our labourers the work that is to be performed upon this timber, from the first and roughest work of chopping and plank sawing to that of planing. That is our intention. We shall not however, fully succeed, for even the present high duties do not completely protect us on the Upper Rhine."

The Reichstag applauded the Chancellor's proposals, and the higher tariff was sanctioned by 199 against 105 votes on May 13th. By another customs measure passed on March 3rd of the same year Bremen followed the example of Hamburg, and agreed to cease being a free city. The independence of the Hanseatic towns as to customs administration had long been recognised as untenable, and their disfranchisement and embodiment in the *Zollverein* followed the re-establishment of the Empire as a matter of course. The end of the Free Towns of Germany came in 1888, but Hamburg and Bremen both had a liberal indemnity in the shape of imperial gold, which has been or is being used in the development of their harbour accommodation. It remains to be added that a still further increase of the corn duties had to be asked for in the winter of 1887. Early in that year the Prussian Government was appealed to in the Diet to urge the Imperial Government to afford agriculture greater protection. The Minister of Agriculture, Dr. Lucius, in reply, acknowledged that the revenue from the corn duties had increased from fourteen to thirty million marks, but he added, "The duties have been of little use to agriculture." Before the year was out the duties were increased, some a hundred per cent., for the third time in eight years. A Liberal journal reminded the Chancellor that the duties were now far higher than he in 1879 believed the "maddest agrarian" capable of raising them, and it commented pathetically upon this piece of political irony: "Times change, and duties with them."

Has Germany's protective system succeeded? This work does not profess to be a history of trade or even of trade movements. It would, therefore, be palpably foreign to the purpose to enter fully into the subject of commercial development in Germany during the past ten years, during which the Free Trade principle has been more and more abandoned. Several years ago it might have been difficult or impossible to prove or disprove the contention of the Protectionists that the economic interests of the country have benefited by the policy inaugurated in 1879.

Controversy as to the wisdom and expediency of that policy was then far acuter than it is now. Party polemic was more excited and an objective judgment was harder of attainment. Now, however, the question can be viewed with more of the historical coolness and impartiality which are so necessary to the formation of fair and correct opinions. The evidence at disposal, both *pro* and *con*, has greatly multiplied ; and where formerly there was little more than speculation to depend upon, there is now a large storehouse of fact. There can be no doubt whatever that the revision of Germany's economic system has tended to encourage her industry and to increase her trade. Prices on the whole are hardly higher, owing to technical improvements and other factors which tend to reduce the costs of production, while on the other hand the position of the workman as to wages and conditions of labour is distinctly better. Agriculture, on the contrary, has experienced little or no positive benefit. Instead of increasing, prices have fallen still lower. The Protectionists maintain, indeed, that without higher duties the prices of agricultural produce would have been less remunerative than they are now ; but this is not a necessary deduction, and in any case it cannot safely be assumed that the continued downward tendency thus presumed would have been a consequence of foreign competition. It would be an easy matter to quote from scores of Chamber of Commerce reports passages favourable to the present protective policy of Germany, and it would also be easy to find a large amount of contradictory testimony in similar reports. On the whole it would appear that while many industries have undoubtedly experienced great benefit from protection, others have suffered corresponding injury. Thus the Düsseldorf Chamber of Commerce reported several years ago : " We can, on the authority of a searching investigation made in industrial circles, assert with satisfaction that the influence of the customs tariff has on the whole been favourable to the branches of industry affected by it in this district. The balance-sheets of the larger establishments, as well as the increase of workpeople, afford ample evidence of this." On the other hand it was found that industries relying upon foreign countries for their raw material and half-manufactured goods suffered greatly, though increased sales and technical improvements were gradually enabling them to overcome their difficulties.

In 1887 the Association of German Iron and Steel Manufacturers, already mentioned, instituted inquiries into the number of workpeople employed and the wages paid by the concerns it embraces both before and since the re-introduction of the iron duties. The results were found to be very remarkable. Two hundred and thirty-three large iron and machine works employed 124,262 workpeople, receiving 7,681,291 marks wages monthly (an average of 61·83 marks per head), in January, 1879. In the same month of 1887 these works employed 162,320 workpeople, or 38,058 = 30·6 per cent. more, and paid them 10,740,056 marks (66·17 marks per head), or 3,058,765 marks = 4·34 marks per head more. Taking the year 1886, the wages of the workpeople—boys and men included—were 52·08 marks a head more than before the return to protection. That these higher wages could well be paid was proved by the fact that while the concerns alluded to made in 1878-79 profits equal to 2·15 per cent. of their share capital, the profits in 1885-86 were equal to 3·94 per cent.

One swallow does not make summer, and one testimony to the favourable effects of protection in Germany would not be conclusive. But evidence on the point is abundant. An unprejudiced mind cannot but acknowledge that, owing to the peculiar economic position of Germany in the last decade, protection was eminently calculated to stimulate and support her industries and commerce. In technical matters on the one hand, and in practical experience and genius for business on the other, Germany was far behind older rivals like England and France. She was only beginning to force her way into foreign markets, while she was yet a great consumer of the productions of other countries. In 1878 the import of industrial articles alone was 570 million marks ; but after the introduction of the new tariff the reduction in the first year was to 395 millions, or 31 per cent. less; while during the same period the industrial exports rose from 1,026 to 1,368 millions, or 33 per cent. more. Unlike England, Germany had industries to create, trade to build up, and she determined to defend herself against the skill and enterprise of older countries during the period of her industrial juvenescence by submitting herself to the leading-strings of protection until she could with assurance and safety walk alone.

CHAPTER VI.

THE STATE AS MONOPOLIST.

WHEN specifying in 1869 the articles which he regarded as most fitted to bear high taxation, Prince Bismarck included in the list tobacco and brandy. Of these two articles the Chancellor has within the last few years endeavoured to establish a State monopoly. His efforts have so far failed completely, but we have his own assurance that he does not despair of ultimate success. It becomes now necessary to review his State Socialistic policy in regard to production, manufacture, and trade.

The principle of nationalisation (*Verstaatlichung*) was first introduced in modern Prussia by the purchase of railways, and this was so gradual that it can scarcely be said to have ever come before the country as an entire innovation. The State began by helping shaky railway companies; then it proceeded to buy and build lines for itself, until the acquisition of railways by the State became a recognised and legitimate part of national policy.

State ownership of railways began more than a generation ago in Prussia, but such State connection with commerce as is involved in the tobacco or brandy monopoly was not heard of until a comparatively few years ago. Prince Bismarck's early speeches make no mention of this form of State Socialism. He has, however, stated that his mind was made up on the question of a tobacco monopoly as long ago as 1867. It was in 1878 that the idea which had been revolving in his head so long first found expression.

Speaking in the Reichstag on February 26th of that year on a bill for the increase of the tobacco duties, he said bluntly, "I do not deny, and do not regard it as superfluous—even though doubts have been expressed as to whether there are monopolists in our midst—to avow openly, that I am aiming at a monopoly, and that I only accept this measure as transitional." This admission produced little short of a sensation both within and without the Reichstag. It was like a bolt from a clear sky. A part of the House was opposed to sanctioning the further taxation of tobacco ; most of the members were flattering themselves with the thought that if they voted the Chancellor the duties he asked they would be deserving well both of him and their country. Yet here they were told that the taxation of tobacco, however high they consented to screw it up, would only be regarded as a make-shift measure, for the State hoped sooner or later to take the entire industry into its own hands. From that day to the present the air has never been free from monopoly projects and rumours of them.

Prince Bismarck's attachment to State undertakings of this kind is primarily based on financial reasons. The monopoly appears to him the best means of raising revenue upon an article which can with justice be saddled with heavy taxation. At the same time he holds that the State is likely to be a better and more conscientious trader than the private undertaker, whose ends begin and end with gain. From the social standpoint, too, he predicts good results from the appearance of the State as an employer in spheres of industrial activity upon which a great number of people are dependent for their livelihood. When it was objected in the Reichstag in 1882 that his monopoly projects savoured of Socialism, he did not deny the imputation, but welcomed it, observing : "Many measures which we have adopted to the great blessing of the country are Socialistic, and the State will have to accustom itself to a little more Socialism yet. We must meet our needs in the domain of Socialism by reformatory measures if we would display the wisdom shown in Prussia by the Stein-Hardenberg legislation respecting the emancipation of the peasantry. That was Socialism, to take land from one person and give it to another—a much stronger form of Socialism than a monopoly. But I am glad that this Socialism was adopted, for we have as a consequence secured a free and very well-to-do peasantry, and I hope that we shall in time do something of the sort for the labouring classes. Whether I, however, shall live to see it—with the general opposition which is, as a matter of principle, offered to me on all sides, and which is wearying me—I cannot say. But you will be compelled to put a few drops of social oil into the recipe which you give to the State—how much I do not know. . . . The establishment of the freedom of the peasantry was Socialistic ; Socialistic, too, is every expropriation in favour of railways ; Socialistic to the utmost extent is the aggregation of estates—the law exists in many provinces—taking from one and giving to another, simply because this other can cultivate the land more conveniently ; Socialistic is expropriation under the Water Legislation, on account of irrigation, etc., where a man's land is taken away from him because another can farm it better ; Socialistic is our entire poor relief, compulsory school attendance, compulsory construction of roads, so that I am bound to maintain a road upon my lands for travellers. That is all Socialistic, and I could extend the register further ; but if you believe that you can frighten any one or call up spectres with the word 'Socialism,' you take a standpoint which I abandoned long ago, and the abandonment of which is absolutely necessary for our entire imperial legislation."

In the same year that Prince Bismarck for the first time declared openly for the tobacco monopoly, a commission was appointed by the Imperial Government to investigate the general subject of tobacco taxation, including the question of monopoly. The eleven members of the commission included eight State officials and three experts, one representing tobacco cultivators, another tobacco manufacturers, and the third tobacco traders. By eight votes to three the commission reported against a monopoly. Even the commissioner delegated by the Prussian Ministry of Finance condemned it. The result was that the Government contented itself with higher taxation for the present, and this was granted in 1879, at the same time that the customs tariff was revised. But although the Chancellor had suffered a reverse, the anti-monopolists were thoroughly alarmed, and without delay they took steps to secure an emphatic declaration from the Reichstag on the subject. On April 28th, 1880, the Radical leader, Herr E. Richter, asked the House to say by resolution that "the further increase of the tobacco duty or the introduction of a tobacco monopoly is economically, financially, and politically unjustifiable." This resolution was rejected, but an amendment, less severe in tone though equally decided, was adopted by 181 votes against 69, asserting the Reichstag's adhesion to the principle of taxation laid down by the customs and excise laws of the previous year, and calling upon the Government to abandon definitely the idea of a monopoly. In spite of this Prince Bismarck in the following February convened the Prussian Economic Council[1] (*Volkswirthschaftsrath*)—a body established in November, 1880, for the purpose of assisting him in the deliberation of measures affecting trade, industry, agriculture, and forestry—and laid before it a full-fledged Tobacco Monopoly Bill. The Economic Council decided in favour of the Government's proposals, and the next step was the mention of the monopoly in an imperial message of November 14th, 1881. This stated : " The further development of the reform in taxation begun in recent years points to the desirability of seeking productive sources of revenue in indirect imperial taxes, in order that the Government may be enabled to abolish oppressive direct State taxes and to relieve the parishes of poor and school charges, additions to the land and personal taxes, and other heavy direct imposts. The surest way to this result is shown by the experience of neighbouring countries to be the introduction of a tobacco monopoly, respecting which we intend to seek the decision of the legislative bodies of the Empire."

The promised measure was introduced in the Reichstag the following spring. The speech from the Crown opening Parliament stated : " Amongst the objects suitable for taxation by the Empire, tobacco takes a prominent place. Opinions do not differ as to this, but as to the form which higher taxation should take, and a decision will have to be obtained by legislation. The majority of the Federal Governments regard the form of a monopoly as that which best conserves the interests of consumers and tobacco cultivators, while at the same time surpassing all

---

[1] The Prussian Economic Council consists of seventy-five members, of whom forty-five are recommended to the Government for nomination by representatives of trade, industry, and agriculture and forestry (fifteen members each) ; while thirty are called by the Government, fifteen at least of these representing the artisan and labour classes. Election is for five years.

other forms of taxation in productiveness. They would only resort to other proposals if they were compelled to abandon the
hope of obtaining legislative assent to the monopoly." Thus was
the monopoly project ushered into publicity. It must be admitted that the imperial benediction upon the proposal was
not a cordial one, and that the manner of its recommendation to
the Reichstag might have been more urgent. Not a few people
thought that the Government, in essaying the monopoly scheme,
had chosen to ride for a fall. Certainly the lukewarm tone of
the imperial utterances and the suspicion of indifference which
seemed to show through some of the Chancellor's later references
to the subject acted prejudicially against the project. The bill
on the subject was introduced on May 10th, being based in part
on the experience of France, Austria, and Italy.

It is worth while to inquire what was the extent of the industry
which it was proposed to hand over to the State. Statistics prepared three years before (for the year 1879) showed that there
were in Germany 159,321 tobacco planters, located in 3,490
places, 81,607 producing for their own consumption, while the
total area under cultivation was 1,799,722 ares. In the manufacture of tobacco 15,028 businesses were engaged (including
Hamburg and Bremen, then out of the Customs Union), employing 140,775 persons, 99,704 in manufactories, and 22,301 in
the house industry. For the sale of tobacco there were in 1877
no fewer than 7,898 businesses of a large kind, with 359,275
businesses where the sale of this article was not the exclusive
trade. Vast as the tobacco interest was, the revenue accruing
to the State in taxation was inconsiderable. Up to 1879 tobacco
had yielded 0·34 mark (about 4*d.*) per head in taxation in Germany, though the amount in France was 5·68 marks, in England
4·86 marks, in the United States 4·36 marks, in Austria 3·41
marks, and in Italy 2·53 marks ; and yet, excepting Austria alone,
Germany had the greatest consumption per head. No wonder
that Prince Bismarck should have declared in 1881, " Tobacco
must bleed more than it has hitherto done." He now proposed
that it should bleed to the extent of £8,000,000 a year, the net
proceeds of the monopoly being estimated at 163,673,167 marks.
The bill, if carried, would place in the hands of the State the

entire production, manufacture, and sale of tobacco.[1] It was a measure of State Socialism which frightened some of the warmest of the Government's supporters. As for the Radicals they were in arms instantly. On May 10th they proposed an amendment to the bill declaring that " after the large increase of the tobacco duty caused by the law of July 16th, 1879, any new troubling of the tobacco industry by further alterations in taxation are inexpedient, and therefore the increase in the tobacco tax contemplated in the speech from the throne of April 27th is not less unpermissible than the introduction of the monopoly." This was straightforward enough, but the Radicals made their retort to the Government's proposal more stinging still by adding a rider to the resolution to the effect that if the Chancellor wished to remove inequalities in taxation, he could so by exercising economy in the disposal of the revenue possessed.

Prince Bismarck, owing to indisposition, did not speak on the first reading of the bill, which was referred to committee on May 13th, though everybody knew that it had no chance of success. For this polite and painless method of administering to the monopoly its quietus 162 members voted, while 121 voted for the summary extinction of the measure. Inside and outside Parliament a violent controversy raged, and many sharp things were said and written on both sides. Heinrich von Treitschke, the Prussian historiographer, supported the monopoly because he despised the tobacco industry and all connected with it. " A man in the middle class," he declared, " who does not know what to do with himself and his leisure has only two ways of killing time : he either sells cigars or writes leading articles." But there were not wanting, and that in abundance, prominent men who approved of the Government's proposal from economic as well as financial motives.

The debate on the second reading was opened by the Chancellor on June 12th, the committee having meanwhile rejected the bill by twenty-one votes to three. He stated that the monopoly was not an end in itself; it was a means to an end, that end being the alleviation of taxation, especially the class and school taxes.

---

[1] For an explanation of the bill see Appendix C.

" We have never doubted," he said, " that the monopoly in itself
is an evil, and that in its introduction—as in the introduction of
every new tax, and indeed of every reform—the primary question is, whether there are not other evils in comparison with
which the monopoly is a lesser one.   When this institution is considered on its merits, and without regard to the purpose which it
is intended to serve, it is placed in a disadvantageous and indeed
unjust light.   The monopoly is only a means to the reforms which
the Government is endeavouring to carry out, it is not their end ;
but the financial reforms at which the Imperial and Federal Governments are aiming are rendered difficult by the fact that the
employment of the means is subject to the decision of the various
Diets, and the provision of the means to the resolution of the
Reichstag.   Thus the opponents of the Government have an
advantage here in the Reichstag, for when a grant is asked they
can say, ' We can grant nothing unless the purpose is told us,'
while in the Prussian Diet or in other Diets they may say, ' We
cannot decide upon the use of grants so long as the grants are not
voted.'   It is self-evident that we are sent from Pontius to Pilate,
so that we get no further with our reforms ; and of this difficulty
the Government's opponents have made good use."

Again : " We have proposed the monopoly because we regard
it, after careful deliberation and weighing of the question, as the
best and most expedient means of taxation, and we require its
rejection before we turn to other measures.   We shall never be
frightened into keeping back a measure which we believe to be
rational by the fact that the monopoly is unpopular, and is artificially made more unpopular than it need be by means of elec-
tioneering dodges.   I never ask if a measure is popular—I only
ask if it is rational and expedient.   Popularity is a transient
thing, which is with one thing to-day and with another to-morrow
—a thing which I have both enjoyed and lost, though I have
easily consoled myself in its loss by remembering that I had
done my duty and left the rest to God.   The popularity of a
thing makes me rather suspicious about it than otherwise, and
I am induced to ask myself if it is also sensible."   He held
that the social advantages of a monopoly would be great, for
the position of the workpeople engaged in the tobacco industry

would be improved, since their livelihood would become more certain than it could be when dependent upon the arbitrary whim of private undertakership. He could not understand the logic of the Radicals. They professed the utmost solicitude for the future of the tobacco workers—who would most benefit by the monopoly—yet they never had a word to say for the " hundred thousand workmen in the iron trade who, with their wives and children, fell victims to the Moloch of Free Trade" a few years before. Nor during the introduction of the railway monopoly long ago was the question asked, "What will become of the carters and the innkeepers ? " though that monopoly was worse than the tobacco monopoly, in that it was a private one.

Yet the Chancellor knew beforehand that his project was doomed to rejection, and, like a good diplomatist, he at once took steps to remove the asperity he had excited. " No enmity even if you do reject the monopoly !" he said on the same occasion. "You must not be vexed with us for having proposed it. Indeed, I do not know why any anger should be manifested—as though we had been busy with high treason, the disregarding of all constitutional rights, the breach of the constitution ! When we simply ask you whether you will raise the money needed in this way or in another—for no one thinks of questioning your right of rejecting the monopoly—I do not understand why angry jealousy should be shown on a question which is purely one of utility." Prince Bismarck evidently thought himself that the Government, in proposing the monopoly, had gone a little too far, and he was not surprised when it was rejected on June 14th, the voting being 43 for and 277 against.

Though defeated so signally, the Government professed not to be dismayed, and three years later the Minister of Finance, Herr von Scholz, gave the Prussian Diet to understand that the project had not been definitely abandoned, though the country would not hear of it again for a long time.

The only other attempt which Prince Bismarck has since made to introduce a State monopoly is the equally unsuccessful brandy monopoly project. This was recommended to the goodwill of the Reichstag early in 1886, and the Government pleaded the same motives as in the case of tobacco—social, economic, and especially financial. The Chancellor spoke in favour of the measure on March 26th, and the Radical attack was led by Deputy Bamberger, who declared, "The tobacco monopoly is a little innocent child when compared with the brandy monopoly and its inevitable consequences." The opposition in the country was unmistakable, and Herr Bamberger spoke with reason when he said, "Never have I seen so spontaneous, wholesale, natural, and voluntary a demonstration proceed from the sense and heart of the nation as that which has been directed against this monopoly." The proposal was defeated, and the following year the Government easily induced the Reichstag to increase the taxation of brandy instead.

So far Prince Bismarck has had no success with his monopoly schemes, yet it would be a mistake to suppose that his approbation of the principle involved is confined to tobacco and brandy. He is known to be in favour of a State monopoly of the insurance system, regarding it as contrary to reason that the capitalists who work the insurance companies should be able to fill their pockets at the expense of the community. No doubt his national and compulsory insurance laws for workpeople have helped to convert the Chancellor to this form of monopoly. Perhaps it should not excite surprise that in days when the principle of State intervention has been applied in Germany so extensively, many proposals of an extreme and even extravagant kind are forced on the Government's attention. Such is the proposal that the State should claim a corn monopoly. Passages like the following are not rare in the ephemeral literature with which the State Socialistic era has deluged Germany: "There is no doubt that the entire social question is essentially a food question, and the measures taken must be such as accord with the necessity of the case and with the dignity of the State. Half measures are of no use; radical measures are imperative—hunger must be appeased. This will only be possible when the State takes the corn trade into its own hands and by fixing prices makes an end at once to the usurer and the speculator." Such a reversion to the policy of Joseph in Egypt has not, of course, many sympathisers amongst reasonable people. The influential Association for Social Politics, which numbers among its active members some of the leading political economists in Germany, goes a long way in the direction of State monopoly. One of its resolutions, adopted in 1873, proposes that the State, or at least the province, district, or parish, should supplant private enterprise in all public undertakings, and that companies and individual capitalists should be restricted to "private departments of production." It needs no prescience to say that upon the question of State monopoly the last word has not been said in Germany.

CHAPTER VII.

THE nationalisation of the railways is another measure whose partial adoption marks the conversion of Germany to the principle of State enterprise in the domain of economic activity.[1] Here, again, it is Prussia which has led the way, though her recent policy in this matter is in direct opposition to early practice. The Prussian Railway Law of 1838 laid down the principle—based on the English custom—that the construction of railways should be left to private industry and should not be undertaken by the State, though the latter should retain a wide control, the monopoly of the post, the right of taxation, and the eventual right of purchase thirty years after the opening of a railway on condition of taking over the debt and paying to the shareholders twenty-five times the amount of the average dividend for the preceding five years. During the seven or eight years immediately following the passing of this law, twelve large lines were built in Prussia by private enterprise. Circumstances, however, compelled the Prussian State to depart in time from the policy of non-intervention with which it entered upon the railway era. It became necessary to guarantee interest to the investors in certain railways in order that these might either be completed or carried on profitably. It was, of course, less out of solicitude for the fortunes of individual persons than from regard for the public interest that this responsibility was undertaken by the State, but for whose helping hand railway projects calculated greatly to benefit the community would have fallen on evil days. Up to 1874, when the German

---

[1] The word nationalisation is throughout taken as the equivalent of the German *Verstaatlichung*. It is right to say at the outset that no significance can be attached to the fact that in 1888 the German Government obtained a large grant from the Reichstag for the purpose of strategic railways required for imperial defence, to be built by the Empire conjointly with Prussia.

railway system reached a turning-point, Prussia had paid in sub-
ventions of this kind the sum of 6,908,587 marks (some £340,000).
Annexation brought Prussia the railways of Hanover and Nassau
and the Frankfort part of the Main-Neckar line. The State also
began, about 1848-9, to buy and build; and in one decennial
period, 1866 to 1876, the Diet voted 725,000,000 marks (over
thirty-five and a half million pounds) for railway construction.
In 1875, of sixty important lines in Germany forty-six were
Prussian, and of these eight belonged to the State, eight were
private lines under State management, and the rest were private
lines in private hands. The Bavarian, Saxon, Baden, and
Wurtemberg railways belonged as a rule to the State.

The standpoint of Prince Bismarck on this question was known
as early as 1847, when he spoke and voted in the United Diet,
which met in Berlin, on behalf of the granting of a State loan
to a private railway enterprise. From that time forward, whether
as private deputy or Minister, he never failed, when opportunity
occurred, to promote the close connection of the State and the
railways, always keeping in view the ultimate end of a thoroughly
nationalised system of railway communication. While Germany
was still disunited, his motto as Prussian Minister President was,
"The railways for the State." When, however, the imperial
throne was again raised, his motto became at once, "The railways for the Empire." The annexation of Alsace-Lorraine gave
to Germany the nucleus of an imperial railway system, but the
uniform administration of the lines in the recovered province
only served to throw into greater relief the utter chaos which
prevailed in the rest of Germany. The railways were of half a
dozen kinds. There were, first, the imperial railways. Then
there were the State railways pure and simple. There were
private lines in private hands, and private lines managed by the
State. Some State lines were, on the other hand, managed by
private enterprise, and there were finally lines leased by the
Empire, as in Luxemburg. Had Germany been a single State
instead of a congeries of States, the difficulties arising out of a
plural system of railway management might not have been so
very serious, or at any rate insuperable. But as each of the
many States had its own system—or rather multiplicity of

systems—the confusion created soon came to be recognised as a national disgrace. Prince Bismarck spoke impatiently of the "sixty-three railway provinces" which still divided the Empire he was striving to unify both in word and in fact. "The traveller from Berlin to Karlsruhe," says a writer, "had to pass through the hands of half a dozen independent railway administrations, while upon the sender of a parcel from Königsberg to Metz it was incumbent to calculate the freight of this consignment according to the rates of nearly fifteen hundred different tariffs." In seeking to reduce this chaos to order, to introduce uniformity of administration, the Chancellor had two objects in view. There was the utilitarian object suggested by the interests of commerce, and the convenience of travellers. If the railways were managed more uniformly, their national purpose, as the greatest means of conveyance and locomotion, would be better achieved. Then there was the political aspect of the question. He believed that the nationalisation of the railways would vastly increase the strength and accelerate the unity of the new Empire. The first step taken towards the attainment of his ideal was the embodiment in the imperial constitution of April 16th, 1871, of clauses securing to the Empire very considerable rights in regard to railway supervision. Article 4 says that the railways shall be "subject to the surveillance of the Empire and to imperial legislation." By article 8 a permanent committee of the Federal Council is to be formed for railways, with the post and telegraph and article 41 sets forth: "Railways which are considered necessary for the defence of Germany or for the purposes of general commerce may be constructed for the account of the Empire by an imperial law—even in opposition to the will of those members of the Confederation through whose territory the railways pass, without prejudice to the sovereign rights of the countries concerned ; or private persons may be authorised to construct such railways, and receive rights of expropriation. Every existing railway administration is bound to allow new railways to be connected with its system at the expense of these lines. Legal provisions granting to existing railways the right of injunction against the construction of parallel or competitive lines are, without prejudice to rights already acquired, repealed throughout the entire Empire. Such right of injunction cannot be granted in concessions to be given hereafter." The following article (42) provides for uniform administration: " The Federal Governments undertake, in the interest of general commerce, to administer the German railways as a uniform system, and for this purpose to have new railways constructed and equipped according to uniform regulations." Article 43 says: " Accordingly uniform arrangements for the working of the railways shall be made as soon as possible, and especially shall identical regulations be introduced for the railway police. The Empire shall take care that the railway administrations shall at all times maintain the lines in such a condition as is required by public safety, and that they shall keep them adequately supplied with rolling stock." Article 45 provides that the Empire should have control over tariffs, and that uniform regulations and, as far as possible, uniform rates and charges should be introduced as soon as possible, agriculture and industry to have special privileges. Article 46 contains a characteristic provision: " In case of distress, especially in the event of an extraordinary rise in the price of food, the railway administrations shall undertake to adopt temporarily a low special tariff, adequate to the necessity existing, for the carrying of grain, flour, pulse, and potatoes, the tariff to be fixed by the Emperor on the motion of the Railway Committee of the Federal Council; but this tariff shall not be below the tariff for raw products on the line concerned." Most of these provisions exclude Bavaria, though the Imperial Government has the power to introduce uniform regulations as to the construction and equipment of railways in Bavaria which may be of importance for the defence of the country.

These constitutional provisions allowed the Chancellor ample scope for the legitimate furtherance of his favourite ideas. If the Reichstag and the individual Legislatures were only of his mind, the constitution offered no objection to the transference of all the railways in Germany to the Empire. Could he expect such unselfishness on the part of the States as would prompt them to such loyal renunciation? That was the question which experience had to answer, and the Chancellor soon received a reply which was not to his mind. Particularism on the part of the States, and individualism on the part of political parties, proved obstacles against which his most cogent arguments and his most pressing appeals were futile. The first practical step in the direction of uniformity in railway administration was taken by the establishment of an Imperial Railway Board (*Reichseisenbahnamt*), which came into existence in the summer of 1873. The project emanated from private members of the Reichstag, yet the Government heartily welcomed it. It was stated that at that time there were at least ninety railway administrations in the country, with 1,357 different tariffs. The whole system was a farce. There was everywhere want of plan and system, and as for community of action between railway and railway, or between State and State, it was not thought of. In order to remedy the existing difficulties, a *Reichsamt für Eisenbahnsachen* (Imperial Board for Railway Affairs) was proposed, this authority to control the action of the various administrations, to see that constitutional and statutory requirements were observed, and to pave the way for further legislation in the direction of uniform tariffs. Prince Bismarck said on May 17th: "I welcome this proposal gladly, as one welcomes reinforcements long looked forward to." A Railway Board seemed the very thing that had been wanting to the realisation of his ideal of uniform railway administration, followed by the acquisition of the railways by the Empire, though he did not say so at the time, for had he done so the Board would probably not have been established. Speaking later, he excused his past inactivity in this matter on the ground of ill-health and pressure of State affairs, since he had recognised the absolute necessity for the proposed authority. He was willing to begin with a Court of Complaints, which should deal with irregularities on imperial, State, and private railways, for that would probably force the observance of existing regulations. "Hitherto," he said, "whenever any contravention of the provisions of the constitution has taken place, the imperial authority (the Railway Committee of the Federal Council) has merely been able to write to the Government concerned: 'In your State such and such irregularities exist in the management of the railways: if you will take steps to remedy them, you will be conforming to the constitntion, and be doing the public a favour.' Then as a rule, there was an end of the matter; the Government answered, and there was correspondence on the question, which was only investigated by the parties interested." On June 16th, 1873, the Imperial Railway Board Bill was passed, and the Board soon gave evidence of activity by requiring considerable grants in aid. In March of the following year the Board published the draft of an Imperial Railway Law, the purport of which was to confer upon the new authority far-reaching control over the railway systems of the country. This measure excited no enthusiasm, and the only result of its introduction into publicity was the fall of the first president of the Board, who found that he had undertaken a thankless office. In April, 1875, Herr May-bach, the then president—afterwards Prussian Minister of Public Works—a capable and diligent public official, published another Railway Law, bolder than the first, for it not only laid down the principle of imperial surveillance, but plainly hinted at the transference of the railways to the Empire, meanwhile advising the various States to get possession of their own lines. This proposal likewise failed, and the Chancellor's confidence in his new Board began to waver.

It was evident that tentative measures were useless, and worse than useless. Hitherto the Imperial Government had done nothing which could unduly alarm the opponents of nationalised railways, yet its regard for tender susceptibilities had not been generally reciprocated. Prince Bismarck determined to have recourse to heroic measures. Without reserve or qualification, he would at once propose that the States should hand their railways over to the Empire, and he would begin with Prussia. Prussia had led the way to national unity in the past, and he knew he might appeal to her again with confidence to set to the rest of Germany the example of self-sacrifice, yea, of self-extinction, for the sake of the Empire. On April 26th, 1876, the first reading took place in the Prussian Diet of a bill for the "transference of the State's property and other rights in railways to the German Empire." The Radical party attacked the measure unmercifully, but the Chancellor himself led the defence, and he carried his scheme safely through both Houses. Replying to the Radical leader, Herr Richter, he ridiculed the idea that "the freedom and unity of Germany, the peace of the world, the Eastern question, the financial crisis, and the momentary stagnation in trade" all depended upon "whether the Empire or the Prussian State acquires a few railways more or not, and whether these railways are in the possession of Prussia or the Empire." He had no fear that German liberty and unity would "travel away with the first imperial locomotive." The question was solely one of economics. Besides, he was but endeavouring to make real an article in the constitution which had hitherto been a dead letter.

"The imperial constitution makes very valuable promises to the commerce of the German Empire and to all the subjects of the same in regard to the treatment of the railways. As an official of the Empire, I am responsible for the imperial action directed to the carrying out of the imperial laws, the chief of which is the constitution; and I cannot emulate the light judgment of any important part of the constitution which distinguishes Deputy Richter—in spite of his generally so constitutional views—when he speaks of article 41 of the constitution as of a dead letter, and refers to it in a contemptuous tone, such as I should not dare, as a minister, to employ in speaking of any part of the Prussian or imperial constitution. I recollect that when the constitution of the North German Federation was adopted, neither the Governments nor the bodies which co-operated with them spoke in this tone of any part of it. On the contrary, great hopes for the future—hopes that were certainly too sanguine—were associated with the constitution. I then reckoned more on the initiative of the Governments—one must always observe the development of things before he can properly understand them—I expected that the Governments would regard more seriously the obligations which they undertook ('The Federal Governments bind themselves to cause the German railways to be administered in the interest of a uniform traffic,') and that the Prussian Government especially would do this, since this part of the constitution was drawn up in the Prussian Ministry of Commerce. But I have been completely deceived in this. Then I believed that the constitution of the Imperial Railway Board, as a Board of Control, might remedy matters. Experience, however, has only shown how impotent the

Empire is *per se*, and how strong the territorial State is. The Imperial Railway Board has become an advising, deliberative, petitioning authority, which writes and does very much, without any one taking any notice of it, an authority whose occupation is such that I can with difficulty prevent the excellent officials who have devoted themselves to it from giving way to the discouragement which is connected with all arduous yet unsuccessful labour."

He complained that instead of any advance having been made in the direction of that uniformity and co-operation desired by the constitution, confusion only tended to become worse confounded.

"In regard to railway communication we have arrived at a state of things which has not been peculiar to Germany since the Middle Ages. We have, I believe, in Germany sixty-three different railway provinces—that is, however, saying too little, for they are more independent than provinces, I might call them railway territories—of which perhaps forty fall to Prussia. Each of these territorial governments is fully equipped with the mediæval rights of staple-right, customs and toll, and arbitrary imposts on trade for the benefit of its own private purse—yes, even with the right of arbitrary retaliation. Nowadays we see that railway administrations, without benefit to the railways and the shareholders, and, as it were, as a kind of sport, wage with each other wars which cost much money, and which are wars of power, without financial competition, more than anything else." This was certainly not the ideal sought by the imperial constitution. But how to mend matters? If all railways could not be transferred at once to the Empire, Prussia must take the lead in the movement for consolidation, and must offer to place her railways in the hands of the Imperial Government. "In view of the obligation which we owe to the Empire, I hold it to be our duty, so long as the possibility of doing it lasts, to strive after the strengthening of the Empire, and not promote the power of a 'Great Prussia'—not to allow the strongest State in the Empire, if we can help it, to gain further preponderance in the economic domain as well, but to offer the elements of this preponderance to the Empire. In my opinion, this is the only way in which the imperial constitution can become a reality."

Still, he did not think the Reichstag would be willing to accept such an offer, even if Prussia made it. Were its answer a refusal, however, Prussia would at least have done her duty to the Empire. He did not expect that his ideal of a complete imperial railway system would be attained during his lifetime.

" But let the development be as slow as it may, let the struggles to be undergone be as great as they may, what important achievement has ever been realised except amidst struggles and, indeed, through struggles ? Let them, therefore, be as great and as difficult as they may, we shall not, conscious of the good ends we have in view, be frightened by them, nor shall we be enfeebled and discouraged, for I am convinced that when public opinion has once grasped a right thought—such as I hold this to be—it will not disappear from the order of the day until it has been realised, until, in other words, the imperial constitution, as whose representative I stand before you, has even in the railway article become a reality."

The bill passed and with larger majorities in both Houses than the Chancellor's friends had expected. Unfortunately, however, for Prince Bismarck's ambitious scheme—though not contrary to his expectation—the measure has been a dead letter, for the Empire has not yet thought well to relieve Prussia of her railways. It is with reason assumed that the cause of the deadlock in the Federal Council on the subject is the dislike of the project showed by the Central German States, especially Bavaria, Wurtemberg, Baden, and Saxony, which fear that with transference of their railways to the Empire their political importance would suffer, and Prussia would be further glorified. The immediate effect of the law was to cause the Prussian Government to extend its purchases of private lines. During one Parliament—1879 to 1882—9,500 kilometres of railway were bought and 2,159 kilometres were passed from private into State management, and now the transfer is fast approaching completion.

The Radical party is the only party in the Prussian Diet which has offered an unbroken front to the process of nationalisation. The Conservatives have invariably gone with the Government, while the Clericals, the National Liberals, and the Poles have always been divided, though their overwhelming strength has been on the side of private enterprise.

A German writer has said of the nationalisation of the railways in Prussia that it is a measure which "constitutes one of the most beautiful leaves in the Chancellor's wreath of fame." Certain it is that from the financial point of view, the policy inaugurated—or rather first seriously carried out—in 1876, has proved a great success. The result of the various transactions has been to place in the Prussian treasury millions of marks which otherwise would have gone into the pockets of shareholders, and the taxation of the country has been alleviated to some extent as a consequence. The authority quoted above contends that if the profits made on the State-owned and State-managed railways were to be applied to the redemption of the railway debt, " Prussia would after a few generations possess the property free of interest, and the conveyance of passengers and goods might be cheaper than in all adjacent countries." Prince Bismarck, however, avowedly disapproves of the idea of making the State railway system a mere revenue-raiser. It is unquestionable that he had financial thoughts in his mind when he persuaded the Prussian Diet to commit itself to a policy of nationalisation, but he did not expect from the State railways immediate gain. He said on one occasion :—

" I do not regard railways as in the main intended to be an object of financial competition : according to my view railways are intended more for the service of traffic than of finance; though it would, of course, be foolish to say that they should not bring financial advantages. The surpluses which the States receive in the form of net profits, or which go to shareholders in the form of dividends, are really the taxation which the States might impose upon the traffic by reason of its privilege, but which in the case of private railways falls to shareholders."

The same view is held by the Minister who has up to the present time administered the Prussian State railways with unvarying success, Herr Maybach, who holds the portfolio of public works, and who declared on February 22nd, 1888, that he had always acted on the principle that "the railways should not be a source of revenue nor yet a cause of deficit." As to the general administration of the State railways, he told the Prussian Lower House on February 4th, 1887 :—

"This year we have made a surplus of 51 millions (marks) beyond the amortisation of three quarters per cent., and next year we expect a surplus of 49 millions, which can be applied to other State purposes. Last year we were able to make a surplus which exceeds by 29 million marks the entire interest on the national debt (of Prussia), and we hope next year to make a larger surplus still when we have built several small lines in order to complete the railway network. This year we have laid aside 784,500 marks for the improvement of the salaries of the officials of private lines taken over by us—a total of 9,700,000 marks applied to this purpose. Moreover, we have made considerable financial sacrifices in order to give railway employees rest on Sunday. Go through the country and ask the people whether or not the nationalisation of the railways has benefited them. You will hear from the overwhelming majority a loud 'Yes.' (Loud applause from the Conservatives.) When, after a few years, we have completely surmounted the difficulties of transition, we shall be able to tell what the State railway administration can do. I am not altogether dissatisfied with what it has done already, but I think it will do better still."

That on the whole Prussia is well satisfied with the change from private to State railways admits of no doubt. It may not be that the interests of industry and commerce always receive the consideration which they deserve, but a sincere desire is manifested by the administration to manage the railways at once efficiently and economically. English residents and travellers in Germany may often wonder that in railway and other branches of government, public convenience is not in every detail made the loadstar of official ambition; but it must be remembered that public opinion does not carry the same weight in Germany as in England, nor does it make the same pretensions which it rightly asserts in a country where *vox populi* is held to be equivalent to *vox Dei.*

The objections raised to the nationalisation of the railways in Germany—and they may be supposed to apply, as a rule, to other countries—are partly political and partly economical. It is held that excessive centralisation is an evil. In the case of Germany this objection must be allowed to carry with it considerable force; for it cannot be doubted that from stress of circumstances, apparently admitting of no check, the strengthening of the Empire is tantamount to the strengthening of Prussia. With every augmentation of imperial institutions, Prussia has been thrust into greater prominence. Despite the Chancellor's natural contempt for Particularism, it is not to be wondered at that the secondary States should object to losing the last remnants of individuality which remain to them under the new order of things. Then, too, there is the argument, of which the Radicals by preference make the most use, that the institution of an imperial railway system would place in the hands of the central Government a dangerous accession of political power. In the first place, the railways might be made an effective weapon with which to fight the constitution as personified in the elected Reichstag. Hitherto the Government has been kept under control by the simple expedient of Parliament maintaining a tight hold of the purse-strings. The idea of making the Government financially independent of the Reichstag has always been unpopular with a majority of the House, and in every new grant of taxes care has been taken that the Empire should be compelled to appeal to the individual States for matricular contributions in order to meet the last few millions of its annual bill. If, however, the railways of the country were handed over to the Empire, the great revenues attainable might be used—unless the constitution were modified—to secure for the Government greater freedom from Parliamentary control than might be desirable. A further objection is, that the institution of imperial railways would vastly increase the number of State officials, and thus, again, the Government would be given a dangerous amount of political influence in the country. Prince Bismarck once objected to the establishment of an Imperial Insurance Office, in connection with the compulsory insurance of workpeople, as an undesirable extension of bureaucracy. Here, however, his critics point out, is a far greater application of the bureaucratic principle. In the absence of Parliamentary government the official classes recognise only one control, that of the Executive, in other words of an authority totally independent of Parliament, because appointed by and responsible in the first instance and the last to the Emperor. Naturally State servants throw all their influence, both individ-

ually and officially, in the scale of the Government, and independent political parties are always placed at a great disadvantage.
By the political power which would accrue by the nationalisation
of the railways, the Government would be able still further to
exercise pressure in election times with a view to securing a
tractable House of Deputies. The Radicals are strong on this
question. They grant that the Railway Minister, Herr Maybach,
declared some time ago that "railway officials must hold aloof
from all political agitations and from political manœuvres ; otherwise we should have officials discharging their duties according to
party colour, and that we will not have." Yet they contend that
this principle is continually ignored, and that officials, high and low,
use their positions for the promotion of party interests. Finally,
there is the objection that the nationalisation of the railways takes
from private enterprise a legitimate sphere of economic activity.
Those who hold this view say that the intervention of the State in
the economic domain should be exceptional, and that no department of commercial life where private individuals or companies
can operate with advantage to the community should be invaded,
much less monopolised, by the State. They contend, too, that by
abolishing competition the interests of the public run a chance of
being neglected. The State is not susceptible to those motives of
self-interest which are the spur of private enterprise. It is likely to
do less what the public may wish than what is pleasing to itself, that
is, to the handful of officials who form the administration. The
argument that the State is not well fitted to manage the railways
economically may be passed over, as it is a question less of theory
than of fact, and the results of the nationalisation of the Prussian
lines so far afford little encouragement to those who take this
ground of objection.[1] These are a few of the reasons advanced
against the carrying out of Prince Bismarck's project of an imperial
railway system. The truth is certainly not to be found entirely
on one side or the other. Great allowance must be made for
national characteristics, national training, national traditions, and

---

[1] For a trenchant critique adverse to imperial railways from the financial
standpoint, see Moritz Mohl's " Die Frage von Reichs-Eisenbahnen " (Stutt-
gart, 1876).

national habits. In Germany the principle of individualism has never attained the acceptance which it enjoys in England, and the change there from private to State railways cannot be said to have occasioned anything like a shock in economic minds. As a matter of fact, though the *pros* and *cons* of State railways are still greatly discussed in Germany, State lines are now the rule and not the exception in that country. The development of the future is the conversion of the State railways into imperial ones. Prussia has already declared for this measure, and having shown the rest of the States the way, there is little reason to doubt that, whether for good or ill, they will eventually follow where she has led.

A few words only are called for by the post and telegraph system of Germany. Both post and telegraph are imperial institutions, except that Bavaria and Wurtemberg are by the constitution (article 4) secured considerable independence of administration. The surplus on the operations of the post and telegraph go to the imperial treasury, and are applied towards the liquidation of the ordinary expenditure. The Post Law of 1871 forbids the transmission of letters and newspapers, etc., from one place to another except through the imperial post, but the private town post is not prohibited. The consequence is, that in a number of large towns one or more local posts exist for the delivery of letters, printed matter, and general consignments within the urban district. In Berlin especially the imperial post has suffered severely from this local rivalry, but so far no amendment of the law has been proposed. Several years ago at least three city posts, carried on by companies and, it must be confessed, worked very admirably, existed at the same time. A law of December, 1875, supplemented the original Imperial Post Law by introducing numerous clauses intended to bring the post and the railway into accord. The law makes great demands on the railways of the country in the interest of public convenience. Germany is acknowledged to be in the very van of countries so far as enlightened postal arrangements are concerned. It was largely owing to her initiative that the *Weltpostverein*, or International Postal Convention, was established in 1874, this invaluable institution coming into active existence in July of the following year. The

Emperor William I. had as early as 1868 endeavoured to bring European countries into postal union, and but for the Franco-Prussian war the international "work of peace," as the union was called, would have been completed sooner than it was. Dr. von Stephan, Germany's sagacious Postmaster-General, had a good deal to do with the introduction of this beneficent agency of civilisation. Though Germany has not yet a uniform postal system, this desideratum is only a matter of time, and the postal legislation is at any rate the same for the whole Empire—a vast improvement on the state of things which prevailed in 1857, when there were seventeen different postal administrations in Germany. As the telegraph and post go hand in hand in Germany as in other countries, special reference to the former is not necessary.

CHAPTER VIII.

THE special legislation which Prince Bismarck has either passed or proposed for the benefit of the working classes has taken two distinct directions. On the one hand he has endeavoured by suitable measures to make the lot of the factory operative and general workman, whether industrial or agricultural, more tolerable, and on the other he has aimed at improving the social condition of the artisan, while restoring his craft to its former efficiency and dignity. Prince Bismarck once compared the social reforms contemplated in this domain with the land reforms introduced by Stein and Hardenberg. What was done for the peasantry after the Liberation War, the new Empire desired to do for the industrial classes. "To this tendency," he added, "*laissez-faire*, the abandonment of the weak to their own resources and to private help, is in diametrical opposition."

I. REVERSION TO THE GUILD SYSTEM.

It is advisable to deal first with measures and movements which have had for their end the improvement of the position of handicrafts and of the artisan, since substantial results have here been achieved. Industrial freedom (*Gewerbefreiheit*), the right of the individual to follow the calling of his choice, was virtually universal in Germany before the North German Trade Law of 1869 became an imperial statute. Prussia, as usual, took the initiative. As early as 1811 the Stein and Hardenberg laws dealt a fatal blow at the guild system, by abolishing guild privileges and making it easy for a man to follow the trade he desired. The movement towards industrial freedom grew in favour until the Prussian Trade Law, passed in 1845, practically recognised the institution as inevitable and unassailable. The political troubles of 1848 and 1849, however, led to a partial reaction. Conscious of its strength, the Brandenburg-Manteufell Ministry of 1849 introduced master examinations, the preliminaries to which were three years of apprenticeship and a like period of journeymanship, with journeyman examinations. On this occasion Bismarck, then a private politician, spoke in the Prussian Parliament in favour of compulsory guilds as a remedy for over-production and as a guarantee for the maintenance of the artisan class in prosperity and efficiency. But the innovation was contrary to the spirit of the time, and it did not work well. The examination never became regarded as of practical value, and the principal part of the proceeding, where it was observed, was the payment of the prescribed fees. The present leader of the Radical party in the Reichstag has recorded : "When in 1861 I held the office of a Landrath, the Ministry of the day addressed a question to the authorities as to whether and how the Trade Law of 1849 had succeeded. Reports lay before me from seven mayors, mostly urban, which differed considerably ; some could hardly estimate highly enough the blessing of the Trade Law, while the others raised critical doubts. I went to the bottom of the matter, and soon found that the entire Trade Law of 1849 had never been introduced in this district. At first an attempt was made to establish examination committees, but it was not possible to maintain the examination system. No one was any longer examined in the district, and no one applied to be examined. In the entire district there was not a single person legally qualified to build houses, though a large amount of building was carried on." [1] In time the demand for the legislative recognition of industrial freedom became so general that the legal restrictions were first ignored and then abandoned, and finally the principle was embodied in the North German Trade Law of 1869.

Before that law was passed all sorts of antiquated commercial privileges, monopolies, and restrictions existed, and their abolition had long been greatly desired. In Mecklenburg, for instance, the old soke-mill retained the exclusive right of corn-grinding. The towns of the duchy could require rural alehouse-keepers to buy their beer within a radius of two miles, and to buy the beer used at baptisms, marriages, and burials at the nearest towns,

---

[1] Speech made by Herr Eugen Richter at Berlin, February 11th, 1881.

while private brewing in the country might be prohibited by the towns. The same exclusiveness formerly existed in regard to horse-shoeing, chimney-sweeping, and flaying. In Reuss j. L. a monopoly in music-playing in public places was granted, and the inestimable privilege of collecting rags was enjoyed by an outside paper manufacturer. In Waldeck there were monopolies in shaving, hair-cutting, and whig-making. Prussia, however, was on the whole free from the old monopolies and privileges.

Early in the seventies, however, another reaction in the direction of guilds began. Artisans had suffered seriously by the development of the factory system, which took their livelihood away, and attempts began to be made to secure the prosperity of the few, where the many could no longer maintain a thriving existence, by reintroducing something of the monopoly and exclusiveness of old. All sorts of measures were proposed by the friends of the guilds, such as the high taxation of machinery, restriction by law in the number of apprentices which an artisan might have, the provision of technical schools for the instruction of apprentices, and the inevitable examinations and certificates of capacity. The Government was not slow to lend its support to the guild movement, and in 1878 it introduced an amendment to the Trade Law, the object of which was to help artisans to compete more successfully against capital and the factory, and this was to be done by the reorganisation of the voluntary guilds, which were to be charged with important functions in regard to the training of apprentices, etc. From that time the Trade Law has been amended nearly every year in the interest of the guild system, the principal amendments being those of 1881, 1884, and 1886.

The avowed object of the various modifications to which industrial freedom has been subjected by law in Germany during the last ten years is the protection of the artisan class against the growing power of capital as represented by the factory system. The idea is to promote *esprit de corps* and self-respect amongst workpeople by their organisation in trade societies, and to ensure better and more conscientious work by the systematic training of apprentices and their later examination for proof of efficiency before the stages of journeyman and master can successively be entered upon. The Trade Law so far has been amended in the

following among other essential matters. Restrictions are placed
upon the right of artisans who do not belong to guilds to employ
apprentices. A guild is given the power of absolutely forbidding
such artisans from engaging apprentices. Various agencies may
be introduced for the benefit of apprentices and journeymen—such
as technical schools and classes for the former, and night-quarters
(in case of travel) and labour offices for the latter—and to the
maintenance of these even those artisans who refuse to join guilds
may be compelled to contribute, it being taken for granted that
they will indirectly benefit by the establishment of such institutions. The demands of the guild party go a good deal further
than legislation yet goes. They will not be satisfied until guilds
are made compulsory institutions, and until examination and the
taking out of certificates of proficiency are incumbent upon
journeymen and masters alike. Already the leading clause of
the Trade Law is virtually meaningless so far as liberty of action
is concerned. It says, "The carrying on of an industry is permitted to every one, save in so far as exceptions and restrictions
are provided for." But so numerous have the "exceptions and
restrictions" become, that a Radical journal some time ago compared this clause of the Trade Law to the announcement of a humor-
ous journal, which said, "This newspaper appears daily with the
exception of week-days." In other words, industrial freedom is
no longer the rule in Germany. This result has not, however,
been arrived at without deliberation and intent. Encouraged and
supported by the Conservatives and the Catholics, the Government has voluntarily entered upon the path of reaction, hoping
that the artisan class, and indirectly the whole community, will
benefit as a consequence. In 1877 a member of the Ministry
announced in the Reichstag that the Government "intended to
adhere to the principle of industrial freedom." That ground has,
however, been definitely abandoned.

It is self-evident that the guild movement has always found in
the Radicals uncompromising opponents, inasmuch as it destroys
the principle of industrial freedom. They deny that the adoption
of this principle has injured handicrafts, and point to the greater
skill of the modern artisan as evidence to the contrary. The
guild system they regard as an artificial prop which will afford

handicraft no substantial assistance, and they especially object to the application of compulsion, and condemn as unjust the power given to guilds to compel non-members to contribute towards the guild costs. The Government, on the other hand, is determined to develop the guilds still further, and a speech 'from the throne of as late date as November 25th, 1886, declared it to be an imperial duty to give these trade organisations support with a view to the restoration of a vigorous artisan class. Up to the year 1886 no fewer than 9,185 guilds existed in Germany. In Berlin, the most Radical city in the country, nearly half the artisans belonged then to guilds. The total number of artisans was 35,330, of whom 13,249, employing 31,988 journeymen and 7,554 apprentices, were organised in guilds. While, however, the Government has during the last few years passed many industrial measures which can fairly be regarded as reversing the established order of things, some of its proposals in this domain have met with universal approbation, and one of these is the Board of Arbitration for trade and industrial questions, composed half of employers and half of employees.

II. Employers' Liability and Industrial Insurance before the New Era.

In considering the questions of employers' liability and the insurance of working people it is necessary to remember that, when dealing with the period preceding the State Socialistic era, we have to do with many systems because there were many independent States. The questions need only be treated generally here, as underlying principles interest us more than actual practice.

To refer first to sick insurance. The systems in vogue in North and South Germany were different. In the South German States it was usual for the parishes to levy a small insurance tax on dependent workpeople and domestic servants, in consideration of which maintenance and attendance were afforded in time of sickness. This parochial system of industrial insurance was of a very inefficient and arbitrary kind, but it served its purpose for a long time. In North Germany the prevailing system was that of the miners' relief society (*Knappschaftskasse*) as it had existed under Frederick the Great, the distinguishing characteristics of which were the compulsory membership of the colliers belonging to a particular mine and equal premiums by employers and employed. This relief society not only supported its members during sickness and provided them with free medical attendance, but assured pensions in time of indigence, contributed towards funeral costs, and gave assistance to the widows and orphans of deceased members. The *Knappschaftskassen* were diligently promoted by Frederick the Great and his successors, and about fifty years ago a good deal was done by legislative means to strengthen them. So efficient have these societies proved that modern reforming legislation has dealt with them very indulgently.

The principle of compulsory membership in a sick relief society was introduced into industrial legislation in Prussia in 1854, by a law which provided for the establishment of societies for various industries based on local codes of regulations. Entrance was compulsory, as was contribution by employers. Of societies founded on the strength of this law some 5,000 existed in Prussia in 1874, their membership being 800,000, their capital 13,000,000 marks (some £650,000), and their annual revenue 9,000,000 marks (roughly £450,000). In addition there were about 2,000 guild relief societies and many private factory societies. The other North German States for the most part followed the example of Prussia —which had taken the miners' relief society for a model—and in 1875 it was estimated that the total number of relief societies in Germany was 12,000, their membership being 2,000,000, and their capital £3,500,000 to £4,000,000. In 1876 the miners' societies of Prussia alone had 263,688 members; supported 15,710 indigent members, 19,090 widows, and 32,650 children; and paid wholly or partially for the education of 58,548 children; their revenue being £600,000 and their yearly expenditure £560,000. There were also in Prussia in this year 5,239 sick relief societies of various kinds for artisans and factory operatives, though the number decreased nearly a thousand during the following four years. In 1876 a law was passed with the intention of placing the sick insurance societies of the country upon a better footing, and of encouraging voluntary insurance amongst the working classes. But the wishes of the promoters of this law were not realised, and when a compulsory insurance law was introduced in 1882 it was justified by the plea that "Experience has abundantly shown that the universal adoption of sick insurance, which must be characterised as one of the most important measures for the improvement of the condition of the working classes, cannot be effected on the lines of the legislation of 1876."

To be just, it must be admitted that the system of sick relief which prevailed until Prince Bismarck made the State play a prominent part in industrial insurance had worked fairly well on the whole in the principal States. It had not proved effective in every trade and industry, but where it operated a good work was undoubtedly done. Such praise cannot, however, be bestowed upon the old system of accident insurance. Here the law was faulty and insufficient, and the protection given to the working classes was very limited and precarious. As early as 1838 Prussia passed a law imposing upon railway companies and administrations nominal responsibility for the accidents which happened to their employees, save in the case of the latters' neglect and blame. But the companies had a knack of escaping liability. Either they contracted themselves out of the Act, or they introduced into their regulations provisions which effectually checkmated the purpose of the law. Where employees claimed compensation for injuries, they were generally bullied into silence; or if it came to judicial proceedings, the strong found it easy to oppress the weak. Very late in the day the Government passed an amendment to the law declaring all evasions to be illegal and of no effect, yet even then the railway companies were able to bid defiance to the statute.

In the rest of Germany the position not only of railway employees but of workpeople generally in regard to compensation for accident was lamentable, and so it continued to be until the time came when imperial legislation of a far-going kind could be passed on the subject. Early in 1869 a large body of men employed on North German railways petitioned the Government for greater protection, and their representations attracted great attention at the time. Wages, it was said, were very low for long hours of work—one to two shillings per day of twelve hours—and the conditions of work were both exhausting and dangerous beyond the rule of English and other foreign railways.

Statistics of that period show, indeed, that the lives of Prussian railway employees were, on the whole, culpably trifled with. While in 1864 Prussian railways only 'carried one-seventh the number of passengers carried in England, with one-fourth the amount of merchandise—the mileage being less than one-sixth that of England, and the number of trains run only one-twelfth the number in England—as many railway officials of all kinds were killed in Prussia as in this country, and England's roll of accidents to railway employees was not thrice longer than Prussia's.

But not only did railway employees begin to agitate for real legal protection. In industry, too, the movement spread with rapidity. Miners and factory operatives joined hands with their brothers on the railway, and the question soon entered the domain of practical politics. In 1871 a law was passed in the new Reichstag making the owners and conductors of railways, mines of all kinds, quarries, and factories liable for the injuries or death caused to their employees through accidents resulting from the pursuit of their callings, so long as the victims were not themselves to blame. In case of fatality the person or persons liable might be compelled to bear the costs of the medical measures attempted, the costs of burial, the loss caused to the deceased's relatives during eventual illness, and in case the deceased were legally liable to support another or others, the latter might recover the loss thus sustained. In case of accident the compensation consisted of medical costs and the loss of wages suffered during illness or through temporary or permanent incapacity. The law was compulsory, and there was to be no contracting out of it. For a time the new protection thus offered to the working classes promised to be of great benefit ; but as soon as they could decently do it, the employers again conspired to defeat its ends. When a workman claimed compensation, an endeavour was too often—not always—made to prove that he had suffered from his own neglect. Law, too, was costly, and a poor man had no chance in an encounter with a capitalist. When in 1877 protection was given to seamen, new authorities were established in the form of Marine Boards for the purpose of investigating the question of liability in every individual case.

But workpeople generally had only the then existing judicial authorities to fly to, and they were not always possessed of the requisite competence. Demands were made in the Reichstag yearly for the amendment of the law of 1871, but pressure of business compelled the Government—to the satisfaction of the Radicals—to defer further legislation on this subject. When this legislation came it formed part of a grand imperial system of industrial insurance, not only against accident, but also against sickness and against old age and indigence. It will be necessary, in the following chapter, to trace the growth of this unique piece of legislation.

III. Regulation of Factories.

It must be confessed that Prince Bismarck's legislative record under this head is a limited one. The German factory operative, indeed, "never is but always *to be* blest," so far as the beneficence of factory regulations is concerned. At present he is very insufficiently protected by law. The Imperial Trade Law, it is true, contains a number of clauses which might be expected to afford some safeguard against abuses on the part of inconsiderate employers, but these clauses are for the most part futile. They are in many places disregarded at will, and the authorities responsible for their due observance have little to say against the transgressors. It is easy to explain this anomalous state of things. The Trade Law applies to a large Empire, composed of many States having different staple industries and different industrial usages. A code of regulations applicable, for instance, to Prussia may be totally unsuited to the established customs of Bavaria. This is only one of many cases in which the difficulty of introducing uniform laws for the entire Empire has made itself conspicuous. It is, moreover, certain that, during late years at any rate, the Imperial Government has been averse to taking any measures which might render the manufacturer's financial position more unfavourable than Prince Bismarck's exacting series of social reforms—particularly the workpeople's insurance laws—must necessarily make it. Hence the disposition to wink at the breach of some of the regulations laid down in the Trade Law.

To mention several of the defects of this law or of its administration.　Sunday labour is nominally forbidden, but in reality the prohibition is of no effect.　Children under twelve years should not be employed in factories, and those of from twelve to fourteen years may only be employed six hours a day.　"Young people" —from fourteen to sixteen years—may only be employed ten hours daily, and mothers may not return to work until three weeks have passed.　These regulations, and others of the same kind, read very well, but they are frequently and flagrantly disregarded, and one principal reason of this is the utterly inadequate system of factory inspection which is provided for by law.[1]　Factory inspection is a comparatively new institution in Germany, and it cannot be said to have taken root firmly as yet.　Prussia introduced inspection of factories first for Berlin and Silesia in 1874, and then for the remainder of the State.　The kingdom of Saxony followed suit, and finally it was made obligatory throughout the Empire in 1878.　The Radicals called the innovation "police despotism," and there was at first considerable opposition on the part of large manufacturers and ultra-individualists, but this was gradually overcome.　Even now, however, the system is very faulty, especially in regard to the fewness of the inspectors. Moreover, no normal work-time is stipulated, either for women or men, the result being that factory operatives are in general employed during an injuriously excessive number of hours, while even women may be employed during the night.　It is no exaggeration to say that fourteen, fifteen, sixteen, and even eighteen hours a day are often worked in factories.[2]　Then, again, while the Trade Law allows combinations for the purpose of obtaining higher wages, the Socialist Law practically takes away the right of coalition.　Professor Schmoller said in 1888 : "We may doubt whether we possess the right of coalition in Germany."

(a) *Hours of Labour.*

Many attempts have been made of late years to amend the law in regard to the duration of work in factories.　A normal

---

[1] The author here speaks from the results of his own inquiries in Germany, as well as on the authority of the Factory Inspectors' reports, in which abundant evidence of the existence of irregularities is to be found.

[2] See debates in the Reichstag, December 15th, 1881 ; January 14th, 1885, etc.

work-day has been repeatedly demanded not only by the Social Democrats as the right of the individual, but by Conservatives and Catholics as a right and in addition a social necessity. Prince Bismarck has, however, invariably opposed State intervention in the matter. He said on January 9th, 1882 :—

" In special businesses the hours of labour cannot be dictatorially curtailed in all cases. Every business has its ebb and flow. We only need to remember the holidays behind us in order to see this. What business in Berlin has not its flood in December —before Christmas? And so in other businesses there is at all seasons of the year a regular return of ebb and flow. If the hours of labour or a maximum period were to be fixed, not to be exceeded, then at Christmas time, when people readily sacrifice their nights in earning money, an unjust and disturbing interference with industrial activity would take place. But in other businesses, apart from the holidays, ebb and flow occur from the very nature of trade. If at times when there is a large demand for a certain product—let me say coal—the labourers cannot be put to a greater strain than at ordinary times, when coal is offered and cannot be got rid of, and when the shifts have to be so reduced that only three are given to the same men in a week, then the entire mining industry, which depends on the year's trade, suffers. There must be freedom of action, so that with a larger trade more forces may be employed than is the case with a small trade. Then the normal work-day entails the further danger that the maximum hours fixed would in many cases exceed the present number."

Upon the latter point he said on January 15th, 1885 :—

" A maximum work-day would be attended with the danger that every employer would feel justified in going to the maximum, even those who had not formerly worked so long. If it were ordered that fourteen hours—which, by the way, I regard as a monstrous work-day and one which is intolerable—might not be exceeded, the employer who had hitherto, perhaps, only worked ten or twelve hours might say, ' I can legally work fourteen hours.' Therein lies the danger of a maximum regulation. A normal work-day would be extremely desirable if it could only be attained. Who does not wish to help the working-man when he sees him

returning home at the close of the day, tired and needing rest,
when he finds him embittered that this rest is not allowed him
through the imposition of overtime—the rest which he would
rather have than the money he earns by overtime? The man
who has not earnestly wished to help the working-man in his
grievances cannot have a heart at all. But how is it to be done?"
This he confessed he did not know. If the hours of work were
to be reduced 20 per cent., wages would fall to the same extent ;
and what would the working classes do then? At present they
earned just sufficient for their needs, and the reduction of their
wages would mean want and distress, unless, indeed, the State
were to step in and make up the deficit. It was impossible to
expect employers to pay the same wages if the hours of labour
were reduced : that would be to increase the cost of production,
to cripple trade, and particularly to strike a heavy blow at export
industries. Thus there were "rocks on both sides: a Scylla on
this, and a Charybdis on that."

Neither on this occasion nor since could the Government be
induced to take any action. In 1887 a definite bill was introduced in the Reichstag by private members fixing the normal
work-day at eleven hours, except on Saturday and the eve of a
festival, when it should be ten ; but it failed. The peculiar clause
appeared in this measure that when factories had worked less than
the legal maximum all the year round, they might for three weeks
work overtime as long as was required to make up for lost time.
A consequence would have been that workpeople who had for
eleven months worked an hour less than the maximum every day
might during the following month be compelled to work night
and day continuously—a course of servitude which the promoters
of the bill certainly never contemplated.

Equally persistent has been the endeavour to secure for the
women and children employed in factories and other industrial
works greater legal protection. From the year 1881 down to the
present, efforts in this direction have been unceasing. The initiative has invariably been taken by the Catholic and Conservative
parties, sometimes independently, sometimes conjointly; but the
Socialists have not been slow to make far-reaching demands. It
is worth while to glance at the Socialist demands on this question.

A bill which they introduced in the Reichstag in March, 1885, proposed (1) a normal factory work-day of ten hours, except Saturday eight hours, for workpeople above sixteen years; (2) for underground work the maximum day to be eight hours; (3) no work on Sundays and festivals, except in the case of railways and canals, means of communication, places of recreation, and industries where uninterrupted work is necessary; (4) no shops to be open more than five hours on Sundays and festivals, and to be closed then by six o'clock; (5) night work to be prohibited except where expressly sanctioned by the authorities; (6) formation of an Imperial Labour Bureau for the promotion and protection of the interests of labour, and of Labour Boards and Labour Chambers, as well as Boards of Arbitration; it should be the duty of the Labour Boards to supervise industrial concerns; while the Chambers, formed equally of employers and employed, were to interest themselves in questions such as those of wages, prices, customs and excise duties, commercial and navigation treaties, continuation schools, pattern and sample exhibitions, working-men's dwellings, the health and mortality of the industrial population, and economical and industrial affairs in general. This ambitious scheme of the Socialists was courteously referred to a committee of the House, and the world heard nothing more of it.

(*b*) *Female and Juvenile Labour.*

Towards all proposals for the restriction of female and juvenile labour in factories the Government has observed an attitude of benevolent neutrality. Prince Bismarck himself has always favoured the principle in the abstract. He advocated on January 9th, 1882, the exclusion of women from factories from domestic and social reasons. " I regard it as in the highest degree desirable," he said, " if factory operatives could stand upon the same footing as nearly all rural labourers, that, as a rule, women should not go to work, but should remain at home the whole day, with the single exception of the time when in agriculture there is a lack of men, that is, in the various harvest operations. Whether this is possible with factory operatives I do not know, but the wages which the wife earns—be the amount half, a third, or two-thirds of the husband's earnings—are always a supplement to the domestic budget." But the Chancellor's sympathy has not yet taken an active form, in spite of the importuneness of his best friends in the Reichstag. It is clear, however, from the reports of the factory inspectors that the question of female and juvenile labour is an urgent one. The returns for 1886 showed that the employment of both women and young children tends to increase. The number of women employed was 8 per cent. more than in the preceding year. What is worse, women must work the same long hours to which men are subjected, and like them they must, if required, work through the night. As to juvenile labour, the number of children of from twelve to fourteen years employed in factories increased as follows from 1881 to 1886: 1881, 9,347; 1882, 14,600; 1883, 18,395; 1884, 18,865; and 1886, 21,053. An inspector in the Düsseldorf district reported in 1886: "I often found in polishing shops, small weavers' works, and belting works, children from four to twelve years of age who were said not to be working, but were only being looked after by their parents or relatives. In very few cases, however, in spite of the untruth of such representations which was shown by the children's hands being soiled by the material used, was I able to prove that they were being employed." Even worse stories were told of the excessive employment of children in the house industries. A Plauen inspector spoke of children of seven years and less who, besides attending school, were kept to work at home for ten hours a day.

In order to strengthen the hands of the Government, the Reichstag, at the instance of the Clerical and Conservative parties, adopted in the summer of 1887 amendments to the Trade Law raising the minimum age of factory-employed children to thirteen years, with the proviso even then that the school requirements should first be complied with; fixing the maximum work-time for children under fourteen years at six hours, and those between fourteen and sixteen at ten hours daily; forbidding the employment of women in mines, quarries, wharves, smelting, rolling, and iron works, and timber yards; and prohibiting the employment of women in factories by night save in the event of extraordinary stress of work. The Government was also requested to take into consideration the advisability of fixing a maximum work-day for adults. Upon all these points reforming legislation is still, how ever, lacking.

(c) *Sunday Labour.*

One of the most disputed of industrial questions in Germany is that of Sunday labour. The Trade Law of the country, which is virtually a copy of the North German Trade Law of June 21st, 1869—this in its turn being based upon Prussian law—says expressly in article 105 : " Employers cannot require their work-people to work on Sundays and festivals," unless from the nature of the industry (as in the case of the chemical industry) un-interrupted work is necessary. This provision of the Trade Law has, however, been from the first a dead letter, employers having regarded it as meriting infraction rather than observance. What is more, the Government has winked at the disrespect shown for the nominal law, the reason being the impossibility of enforcing legal regulations which do not coincide with the convictions and customs of the community. Since the establishment of the Empire attempts have continually been made by several parties in the Reichstag—particularly the Clericals or Ultramontanes—to induce the Government to abolish Sunday labour. But these attempts, like all definite legislative proposals introduced upon the subject by private members, have always failed, and that signally. The Postal Department did, indeed, make a small con-cession in 1880 by discontinuing one of the two Sunday deliveries of letters then customary in Berlin, while the Prussian State rail-way authorities began to give their employees one Sunday in every three, but the postal reform was abandoned several years ago. The evil did not rest entirely, or even principally, with manu-facturers. Although in some parts of the Empire Sunday labour in factories and workshops was very common, shopkeepers and merchants were on the whole more addicted to the custom. A Sunday Rest Association, established at Bremen in 1880, col-lected returns on the subject from all parts of Germany, and these acquitted most of the large towns of Sabbath desecration so far as mills were concerned, while proving that Sunday employment largely prevailed in workshops, offices, and shops. Another fact established by these returns was the comparative absence of Sunday labour from States or districts in which industry was greatly developed, Saxony, Alsace, and the Lower Rhine being among the illustrations given.

The first serious endeavour to convert the Government upon this question was made in the winter of 1881, when the Clericals called for the amendment of the Trade Law in the direction of less or no Sunday labour. Baron von Hertling had no difficulty in proving that the imperial law on the subject was systematically disobeyed. He quoted from the report of the Wiesbaden factory inspector, who wrote in 1876 : "Even if workpeople cannot legally be compelled to work on Sunday, they are still in many cases defenceless against their employers owing to the interpretation given to section 105 of the Trade Law. In times such as those which we have passed through of late years no labourer can refuse to work on Sunday unless he is prepared to receive the answer that he need not return to his work on the week-day. What this means in the many places where there is but a single industrial concern in which work can be found, I scarcely need point out." The case was mentioned of a large Rhenish manufacturer who kept his employees at the wheel all the year round, Sunday and week-day, with the exception of such high festivals as Christmas Day and Good Friday. At this manufactory prisoners from a neighbouring gaol were regularly employed, but the governor of the prison only allowed them to work six days a week. Convicts enjoyed a free Sunday, but free workpeople were, on pain of money fine, compelled to toil every day of the week. It was, moreover, pointed out that without Sunday labour the hours worked were sufficiently exacting in the textile industry, fourteen and fifteen a day being the rule, and sixteen and eighteen being common. Prince Bismarck manifested great interest in the subject, and replied on January 9th, 1882, in a long speech. " It is," he said, " a tradition of the dynasty which I serve that it takes the side of the weak in the economic struggle. Frederick the Great said, '*Je serai le roi des gueux*,' and in his own way he carried out this precept with strict justice to high and low, according to the manner of the age. Frederick William III. gave to the bond peasantry of his day a free position, and in this it was able—

until a retrogressive movement set in some fifteen years ago—to prosper and become strong and independent. My present master is animated by the lofty ambition to at least give an impetus in his old age to measures which may secure to the weakest class of our fellow-citizens, if not advantages equal to those secured to the peasantry seventy years ago, at any rate a material improvement in their position, and in the confidence with which they can contemplate the future and the State to which they belong." He was himself strongly in favour of Sunday rest for the working-man, yet he would not agree to take the initiative. That must come from the industrial classes. The law nominally forbade Sunday work already, but it was broken because the nation as a whole did not sympathise with it. To pass another law before it could be shown that it was called for would be unpractical and inexpedient. He asked for time, therefore, and promised to institute exhaustive inquiries into the question. So the matter dropped.

In January, 1885, the question of Sunday labour was again raised in the Reichstag, and this time by three parties at once, their proposals being referred to committee. The result of the committee deliberations was that in March the Conservatives and Clericals introduced a joint bill proposing at once to greatly restrict labour on Sundays and festivals, and to promote the formation of trade guilds. Not to be beaten, the Socialists made propositions more stringent still, and the various projects went in the ordinary way to the committee room. This time the committee reported in favour of Sunday rest for factory operatives, journeymen, apprentices, etc., condemned the present law as useless, called on the Government to issue a commission on the subject, and finally suggested the amendment of the Trade Law in the direction of Sunday observance. Replying on May 9th, the Chancellor repeated his approval of the principle at issue, but declined to move until the Federal Council had better data to go upon.

In this way originated a highly important commission which in 1886 and 1887 inquired into the custom of Sunday work in all parts of the German Empire. The results of its exhaustive investigations were published in four volumes, which threw invaluable light not only upon this question but upon the condition of industry and of the working classes generally. It was shown that Sunday work was largely carried on in most trades, both in manufactories and in workshops, and that shops and offices were more frequently open than closed on Sunday. Of course, the views of manufacturers differed widely, though the majority were favourable to less or no work on Sunday. A Saxon employer declared that "besides the manufacturer's greed of gain there is no reason for Sunday work, and all the justification advanced is pretence." On the other hand, many manufacturers—as in the chemical and paper trades—regarded Sunday work as imperative, though even here absolute agreement did not exist. While one Saxon employer wrote : "As I am dependent on water for my engine, and on wind, rain, and sunshine for the drying of my paste-board, I must use them as God gives me them," another con-tradicted this statement by declaring that "technical difficulties can scarcely be an objection to the discontinuance of the Sunday working of paper machines." As a rule the workpeople appealed to declared for one day of rest in the week. " Now we hardly see our children," was the plea of one witness ; and another said that while prohibition of Sunday work would "certainly reduce his yearly earnings by one-fourteenth, on the other hand there would be compensation in the pleasures of a more regular family life." Yet another spoke of the prevailing system as "frightful torture," and the general attitude of the industrial classes proved to be one of desire for a free Sunday and of indifference as to the consequent reduction of wages. The Government did not take immediate action on the question, and the Clericals therefore re-introduced in 1888 the proposals made by the committee of 1885. As yet, however, no legislation has resulted.

The reasons which have hitherto prevented Prince Bismarck from proposing legislation forbidding Sunday labour are two in number. In the first place he regards this as a working-men's question. He is not prepared to abolish Sunday work, or, indeed, to propose any diminution in the hours of labour, at the expense of the employers. If the workpeople are willing to lose the earnings which come to them by reason of Sunday employ-ment, he will consider the advisability of restricting their work to the six week-days. But until he is assured of their readiness to

make such sacrifice, he declines to interfere, though heartily wishful to see Sunday labour abolished.   Speaking in the Reichstag
on May 8th, 1885, he said : " As soon as I am convinced that
the working classes really desire to be protected from Sunday
labour, and will be grateful to me if it is forbidden on pain of
punishment, I shall be glad to promote the matter in the Federal
Council.   But I must have this assurance first."   Then the
Chancellor is loath to make any further attack upon the traditional rights of employers at present, since the several workpeople's insurance laws passed during recent years have entailed
upon them great sacrifice.   While wishful to secure to the working
classes all the legislative protection and assistance they have a
right to claim, he is too far-seeing to carry the principle of State
intervention to such an extent as would endanger the prosperity
of industry.   It is neither to the interest of the State nor of the
working classes that the employers should be laid under social
obligations so heavy as to make it impossible to trade with profit.

"Where is the limit," the Chancellor once asked when discuss-
ing the Sunday labour question, "up to which industry can be
burdened without killing the hen that lays the labourer's golden
egg?   When requirements are imposed upon industry for the fulfilment of State purposes—and the giving to all employees of a
higher measure of contentment, as to which industry may itself be
indifferent, *is* a State purpose—it is necessary very accurately to
know the limit up to which this industry may be burdened.   If
we proceed to work without considering this limit, and it may be
without seeking it, we run the risk of loading industry with burdens
which it may be unable to bear.   No one carries on an industry
at a loss, or even for small profits.   The man who is contented
with five per cent. interest on his capital has a more comfortable
time of it when he confines his attention to the coupon-scissors,
which are never used up, and never fail—it is a clean business.
But the man who incurs risk by investing a large amount of capital
in enterprises whose career no one can foretell does so for the
profit which he hopes to make, for the increase of his future provision for his family.   If this profit disappears a misfortune falls
upon the workman, and one which, in my opinion, is far worse
than the long duration of his work, viz., the danger of destitution,

with the transitional stage of decreased wages. The evil is first felt in the curtailment of wages when the demand for labour is so diminished that instead of the complaint being that too much work is required it is that there is too little, so that only three days' employment are offered for six days' time ; until eventually the industry upon which the workman depended fails, and the difficult problem of complete destitution appears in a menacing form. We cannot overlook the fact that every one of the improvements which we are introducing in the interest of the working classes is a fresh burden upon industry. If we, even without knowing it, reach the limit at which the pressure upon industry becomes no longer tolerable, but the consequences to which I have referred set in, shall we be prepared to give State support to the industry from which we have demanded sacrifices in the fulfilment of State purposes ? "

As the imperial commission on Sunday work has made it clear that a measure of prohibition would not be unacceptable to the country, it is not too much to expect that it will be proposed before long.

[Since the above pages were written the German Emperor's famous rescript proposing an international conference on labour questions—an utterance which does as much credit to his heart as his head, and which increases his reputation for far-seeing statesmanship—has been issued ; and whatever be the fate of his conference plans, the document certainly indicates the lines upon which future industrial legislation will advance in Germany. The rescript of February 4th, 1890, says :—

" Besides the further extension of the scope of the Working Men's Insurance Law, an examination is necessary into the present provisions of the Trade Laws as affecting factory labour with a view to meeting in this direction any complaints or wishes as far as these may be justified. It is the duty of the State so to regulate the duration and nature of labour as to insure the health, morality, and economic wants of the working-men, and to preserve their claim to legal equality. For the promotion of peace between employers of labour and working-men legal measures must be taken to establish regulations which will empower working-men to be represented by delegates enjoying their confidence in the settlement of their affairs, and in guarding their interests in negotiations with their employers or with the representatives of the Government. Such an arrangement would enable the working-men to give expression to their wishes and grievances freely and in a peaceable manner, and would give the authorities of the State an opportunity of informing themselves at all times upon the condition of the working classes, thus keeping in touch with them."

The Emperor followed up this rescript by convening the Council of State in order to consult it upon the questions raised. Addressing the Council on February 14th, his Majesty said :—

" The task for the accomplishment of which I have called you together is a serious and responsible one. The protection to be accorded to the working classes against an arbitrary and limitless exploitation of their capacity to work ; the extent of the employment of children, which should be restricted from regard to the dictates of humanity and the laws of natural development ; the consideration of the position of women in the household of workmen, so important for domestic life from the point of view of morality and thrift, and other matters affecting the working classes connected therewith, are capable of better regulation. In the consideration of these questions it will be necessary to examine with circumspection and the aid of practical knowledge to what point German industry will be able to bear the additional burdens imposed upon the cost of production by stricter regulations in favour of workmen, without the remunerative employment of the latter being prejudiced by competition in the world's markets. This, instead of bringing about the improvement desired by me, would lead to a deterioration of the economic position of the workmen. To avert this danger a great measure of wise reflection is needed, because the satisfactory settlement of these all-absorbing questions of our time is all the more important since such a settlement and the international understanding proposed by me on these matters must clearly rest one upon the other. No less important for assuring peaceful relations between masters and men are the forms in which workmen are to be offered the guarantee that, through representatives enjoying their confidence, they shall be able to take part in the regulation of their common work, and thus be put in a position to protect their interests by negotiation with their employers."

The invitation addressed to the Powers to take part in a conference was readily accepted, but the scope of the deliberations was for some reason or other practically narrowed to the question of female and juvenile work. The principal points in the programme issued from Berlin were : (1) The regulation of work in mines with reference to the question of prohibiting the labour of women and children underground, and to the desirability of restricting the duration of the shifts in unhealthy mines; (2) the regulation or prohibition of Sunday labour; (3) the regulation of children's labour; (4) the regulation of the labour of young people ; and (5) the regulation of female labour. The conference met in Berlin in the middle of March.[1] As the programme contains no proposal for the reduction of the working hours of adult males, it is to be feared that the practical results of the conference will disappoint many friends of the labouring classes. That, however, the Emperor is actuated by lofty motives, and by a strong and sincere desire to better the lot of the toilers, is proved by his frequent utterances during the preliminary deliberations of the Prussian Council of State, which laid down the basis of the conference. His last words to the Council, spoken on February 28th, when it dispersed, were as follows : "I beg you to combat in public the opinion that we are assembled here to find the secret for curing all misery and social ills. We have together loyally sought for such means as will lead to the amelioration of many things, and also for such measures as may conduce to the protection of the workman."]

---

[1] The resolutions adopted by the Conference appear in Appendix D.

CHAPTER IX.

REPLYING once to the accusation made by an opponent in the Reichstag that his social-political measures were tainted with Socialism, Prince Bismarck said, " You will be compelled yet to add a few drops of social oil in the recipe you prescribe for the State ; how many I cannot say." In no measures has more of the Chancellor's " social oil " been introduced than in the industrial insurance laws. These may be said to indicate the high-water mark of German State Socialism. That they are the result of organic development has already been shown. The Sickness Insurance Law of 1883, the Accident Insurance Laws of 1884 and 1885, and the Old Age Insurance Law of 1889 are based upon the principle of compulsion which was introduced into the sick insurance legislation of Prussia in 1854. The laws relating to insurance against sickness and accident were rendered neces- sary by the inadequacy of the existing statutes. The law intended to protect the workman against the ill-effects of a helpless and indigent old age had no prototype in either German or Prussian legislation, yet it followed as a logical consequence, if not of the laws already mentioned, at least of the principles upon which they were avowedly based. After all, the idea of insuring the indus- trial classes against the time of old age and incapacity for work was heard of in Germany long before the re-establishment of the Empire. As early as 1850 a Chemnitz manufacturer proposed in the Frankfort Parliament that the State should levy a tax upon all employers of labour for the benefit of workpeople who had through advancing age or other causes become less efficient, and for the establishment and maintenance of homes for aged and worn-out labourers. The proposal, however, found no support.

I. How the Insurance Laws originated.

Before the Government of Prince Bismarck had promised the trio of insurance laws which are now in operation, a small body of Conservatives in the Reichstag urged the introduction of obligatory insurance against old age and indigence. This was in 1878 and 1879, and the Ministerial reply was not altogether negative. The Socialist Deputy, Herr Bebel, strange to say, advocated in the latter year insurance by the State direct—a principle which two years afterwards the Government unsuccessfully endeavoured to carry into effect. The attitude of the Government in 1879 was thus explained by Minister Hofmann: "The Government accepts the theory that the working-man who has become incapacitated through age, or in consequence of his work, should not be a burden upon the public, but should be provided for by other institutions. It is, however, difficult to say *how*." The debate which took place on this occasion showed the growth of a strong feeling in favour of an extended system of industrial insurance, and all eyes turned to the State for direction in the settlement of what had become a great social problem. In 1881 came the first decided word from the Emperor and his Government upon the subject. The speech from the throne which opened the Reichstag on February 15th, 1881, said :—

" At the opening of the Reichstag in February, 1879, the Emperor, in reference to the [Anti-Socialist] law of October 21st, 1878, gave expression to the hope that this House would not refuse its co-operation in the remedying of social ills by means of legislation. A remedy cannot alone be sought in the repression of Socialistic excesses ; there must be simultaneously the positive advancement of the welfare of the working classes. And here the care of those workpeople who are incapable of earning their livelihood is of the first importance. In the interest of these the Emperor has caused a bill for the insurance of workpeople against the consequences of accident to be sent to the Bundesrath—a bill which, it is hoped, will meet a need felt both by workpeople and employers. His Majesty hopes that the measure will in principle receive the assent of the Federal Governments, and that it will be welcomed by the Reichstag as a complement of the legislation affording protection against Social-Democratic movements. Past institutions intended to insure working people against the danger of falling into a condition of helplessness owing to the incapacity resulting from accident or age have proved inadequate, and their insufficiency has to no small extent contributed to cause the working classes to seek help by participating in Social-Democratic movements."

The duties and functions of the State, as interpreted by the Crown and the Government, were more fully set forth in the *Begründung* which accompanied the first Accident Insurance Bill, bearing date March 8th, 1881.

" That the State," it said, "should interest itself to a greater degree than hitherto in those of its members who need assistance, is not only a duty of humanity and Christianity—by which State institutions should be permeated—but a duty of State-preserving policy, whose aim should be to cultivate the conception—and that, too, amongst the non-propertied classes, which form at once the most numerous and the least instructed part of the population —that the State is not merely a necessary but a beneficent institution. These classes must, by the evident and direct advantages which are secured to them by legislative measures, be led to regard the State not as an institution contrived for the protection of the better classes of society, but as one serving their own needs and interests. The apprehension that a Socialistic element might be introduced into legislation if this end were followed should not check us. So far as that may be the case it will not be an innovation but the further development of the modern State idea, the result of Christian ethics, according to which the State should discharge, besides the defensive duty of protecting existing rights, the positive duty of promoting the welfare of all its members, and especially those who are weak and in need of help, by means of judicious institutions and the employment of those resources of the community which are at its disposal. In this sense the legal regulation of poor relief which the modern State, in opposition to that of antiquity and of the Middle Ages, recognises as a duty incumbent upon it, contains a Socialistic element, and in truth the measures which may be adopted for improving the condition of the non-propertied classes are only a development of the idea which lies

at the basis of poor relief. Nor should the fear that legislation of
this kind will not attain important results unless the resources of
the Empire and of the individual States be largely employed be a
reason for holding back, for the value of measures affecting the
future existence of society and the State should not be estimated
according to the sacrifice of money which may be entailed. With
a single measure, such as is at present proposed, it is of course
impossible to remove entirely, or even to a considerable extent,
the difficulties which are contained in the social question. This
is, in fact, but the first step in a direction in which a difficult
work, that will last for years, will have to be overcome gradually
and cautiously, and the discharge of one task will only produce
new ones."

The first reading of the bill was taken on April 1st. Three
days before this the Chancellor had given the Reichstag an
advance-proof of his views on the question. Speaking of his
general scheme of social and fiscal reform, he said :—

" The end I have in view is to relieve the parishes of a large
part of their poor-law charges by the establishment of an institution, having State support and extending to the entire Empire,
for the maintenance of old and incapacitated people, just like the
institution of accident insurance."

And further :—

" A generation may perhaps be necessary in order to decide
whether the ends I have in view can be attained or should be
abandoned, but the way must be trodden, and I believe that the
parishes—especially those overburdened with poor—and under
certain circumstances the circuits (*Kreise*) as well, would experience considerable relief if the poor-law charges were distributed more justly amongst larger unions than now, and that they
would receive considerable relief, without direct grants in cash,
if all persons requiring relief owing to natural causes, as incapacity or old age, were to be received into an insurance institution
established by the State."

Supporting the proposed law on April 2nd, Prince Bismarck
amplified these views. He said :—

" The domain of legislation which we enter with this law . . .
deals with a question which will not very soon be removed from

the order of the day. For fifty years we have been speaking of a
social question. Since the passing of the Socialist Law I have
continually been reminded by persons in high and official circles,
as well as by others in the popular classes, that a promise was
then given that something positive should also be done to remove
the legitimate causes of Socialism. I have had the reminder in
mind *toto die* up to this very moment, and I do not believe that
either our sons or grandsons will quite dispose of the social question which has been hovering before us for fifty years. No
political question can be brought to a perfect mathematical conclusion, so that book balances can be drawn up; these questions
rise up, have their day, and then disappear among other questions of history : that is the way of organic development."

He held that the State had positive and active functions to
discharge, and that in Christian, monarchical, and paternally
governed countries like the German States the principle of
Laissez-faire was inadmissible. " I have a feeling," he said,
"that the State can be responsible for its omissions," by which he
meant its neglect to afford adequate help and protection to the
weaker of its citizens. He not only demanded for the working
classes insurance against sickness, accident, and old age, but he
asked that the State would bear a fair share of the cost. Industry
could not bear the whole burden, and it would be absurd to try
to make the working-man exclusively liable. So far as the present
measure was concerned it was intended that the insurance premiums should be paid equally by employers, employed, and the
Empire. In proposing a national system of insurance he held
that the State could not fairly entrust the insurance of workpeople
to private adventure. " The corollary of compulsion is, in my
opinion, insurance through the State—either through the Empire
or the individual State : without that no compulsion. I should
not have courage to exercise compulsion if I had nothing to offer
in return. . . . If compulsion is enforced it is necessary that
the law provide at the same time an institution for insurance,
which shall be cheaper and securer than any other. We cannot
expose the savings of the poor to the danger of bankruptcy, nor
can we allow a deduction from the contributions to be paid as
dividend or as interest on shares. . . . According to my idea

of justice, we could not compel insurance in private companies which might go into bankruptcy, even with good management, because of conjunctures or great calamities, and which are compelled to so fix their contributions that dividends can be paid to those who invest their money in the concerns—or at least a good interest with the hope of dividend."

II. The Sickness Insurance Law.

The first accident insurance measure need not detain us long, for it was wrecked. It was intended to apply to railways, factories, and mines, whose employees were to be insured against accident of any kind in an imperial insurance institution, the premiums to be borne by the employers, the insured, and the Empire. The Socialists at once proposed, though unsuccessfully, to extend the measure to workpeople—men and women—of every class, and to throw the premiums entirely upon the employers. While they declared the measure to be but a "bastard form of Socialism," the Radical leader said it was "even worse than Socialism." In spite of much opposition the bill found its way into committee, and there several fatal alterations were made. Imperial subsidy was rejected—the employer having to pay two-thirds and the insured one-third of the premium—and the burden of insuring workpeople was transferred from the Empire to the individual States. Thus amended, the bill was passed by the Reichstag, and by it referred back to the Federal Council, which, however, withheld its assent, the measure thus falling to the ground.

But the question was not permanently shelved. It was referred to in the speech from the throne with which the Reichstag was opened on November 17th of the same year—1881. This imperial message contained a memorable, a historical passage, which has ever since been regarded as the Social Charter of the first Emperor's reign. "In February of this year," ran the famous declaration, "we expressed our conviction that the cure of social ills must be sought, not exclusively in the repression of Social-Democratic excesses, but simultaneously in the positive advancement of the welfare of the working classes. We regard it as our imperial duty to urge this task again upon the Reichstag, and we should look back with all the greater satisfaction upon all the successes with which God has visibly blessed our government if we were able one day to take with us the consciousness that we left to the Fatherland new and lasting sureties for its internal peace and to those needing help greater security and liberality in the assistance to which they can lay claim." The Emperor promised an amendment of the original accident insurance measure and a bill for the extension of the sickness insurance system, and recognised the right of aged and infirm workpeople to "greater State care than has hitherto been accorded them," adding : "The finding of the proper ways and means for the latter is a difficult task, yet it is one of the highest of every commonwealth which is based on the ethical foundations of a Christian national life. The closer union of the real forces of this national life and their combination in the form of corporate associations, with State protection and State help, will, we hope, render possible the discharge of tasks to which the Executive alone would not to the same extent be equal. Yet even in this way the end will not be reached without considerable expenditure."

Before the Government had time to bring in another Accident Insurance Bill the Radicals proposed one of their own. The party had taken fright at the scheme of State insurance, and in order to protect private enterprise and to prevent the further growth of State Socialism in legislation they initiated a measure extending the liability of employers while establishing industrial insurance on strictly commercial and individualistic principles. This measure was referred to committee, but it did not make further progress.

In the spring of 1882 the Government introduced an amended Accident Insurance Bill together with a Sickness Insurance Bill. The measures were combined because one was the natural complement of the other. It was proposed that the organisations to which sick insurance was entrusted should support workpeople for the first thirteen weeks of inability to work, and that afterwards they should be transferred to the accident insurance funds. The Government now abandoned the idea of insurance by the State direct, and Prince Bismarck frankly avowed his conviction that the Imperial Insurance Office contemplated in the former measure was "too bureaucratic." In place of a State central institution were to be introduced trade organisations, based on the principle of mutual liability. Both bills were promptly referred to committee, but only one, the Sickness Insurance Bill, could be disposed of that session. This measure passed the Reichstag on May 31st, 1883, by a majority of 117 votes—216 against 99, the majority consisting mainly of the Radical and Socialist deputies.

The spirit which generally informed the Reichstag in the consideration of this measure was well shown by the words with which the report of the committee opened. "We all approach this proposal," they ran, "with the feeling that it requires and deserves the most serious examination, and that not only our understanding but our heart and conscience should guide us in that examination." The law was promulgated June 15th, 1883, and it came into force December 1st, 1884. Amendments and extensions were introduced in Acts of January 28th and May 28th, 1885, and May 5th, 1886, the last coming into operation on April 1st, 1888, so that now the entire working classes and smaller official classes of the country may be said to be embraced in the sickness insurance system.

III. The Accident Insurance Law.

Reserving an examination of the scheme of sickness insurance thus established, it will be convenient to trace further the career of the Accident Bill. An imperial message to the Reichstag of March 6th, 1884, stated that social-political legislation would monopolise attention during the forthcoming session.

"The Emperor's wish, solemnly and emphatically declared on repeated occasions, to improve by organic laws the economic and social condition of the working classes, and thus to promote amity amongst all classes of the population, has found complete endorsement by the German nation. The deliberations on the Sickness Insurance Law passed last year furnished welcome evidence that the Reichstag is at one with the Federal Council in the consciousness of the importance and urgency of the social reforms contemplated. The next step in this direction consists of legal provision for working people injured by accident during employment, and in case of death for those dependent on them.

Seeing that the Accident Insurance Bill introduced in the spring of 1882 did not receive legislative sanction, it has been subjected to careful reconsideration in the light of the experience derived from past developments of the question. This has led to the modification of the contemplated co-operative organisation of industrial undertakers on the basis of extended self-government, as well as the further participation of the workpeople in the same for the protection of their interests. . . . When the Accident Insurance Bill has become law, it will be our duty to seek to establish, upon a similar basis of organisation, satisfactory provision for workpeople who through age or incapacity have become unable to earn their livelihood."

Prince Bismarck spoke on March 15th, 1884, in support of the new Accident Insurance Bill. He admitted at the outset that the Reichstag was asked to join the Government in exploring a *terra incognita*, and that the difficulties to be encountered would increase the more the progress made. In order to make success more certain it was proposed to begin with an incomplete measure, which should only embrace a section of the great industrial army.

"Yet we do not," he added, "intend to disregard the other branches of industry; we only desire to guard against the danger indicated by the proverb that better is the enemy of good, the danger that when one tries to attain too much he may attain nothing at all. I should like us and the German Reichstag to have the merit of having made at least a beginning in this domain of legislation, and thus of having preceded the other European States. The limitation of the measure is dictated by the consideration that the wider and more comprehensive it is the more numerous are the interests touched, and therefore the greater the opposition on the part of the representatives of these interests, which will be aroused and will find expression here, so that the passing of the measure would be all the more difficult. The extent of the limitation should in my opinion be determined by the extent of the Employers' Liability Act of 1871, for I regarded it as our first duty to remove the deficiencies of the first attempt made in this domain by that law."

He laid before the Reichstag the question, Should the State compel the insurance of, working people? and answering it in the affirmative he drew the conclusion that the State should take insurance into its own hands, and not leave it to private enterprise, which really meant private speculation on the misfortunes of the labouring population.

"The whole matter centres in the question, Is it the duty of the State, or is it not, to provide for its helpless citizens? I maintain that it is its duty, that it is the duty not only of the '*Christian* State,' as I ventured once to call it when speaking of 'practical Christianity,' but of every State. It would be foolish for a corporation to undertake matters which the individual can attend to alone; and similarly the purposes which the parish can fulfil with justice and with advantage are left to the parish. But there are purposes which only the State as a whole can fulfil. To these belong national defence, the general system of communications, and, indeed, everything spoken of in article 4 of the constitution. To these, too, belong the help of the necessitous and the removal of those just complaints which provide Social Democracy with really effective material for agitation. This is a duty of the State, a duty which the State cannot permanently disregard. . . . As soon as the State takes this matter [of insurance] in hand—and I believe it is its duty to take it in hand—it must seek the cheapest form of insurance, and, not aiming at profit for itself, must keep primarily in view the benefit of the poor and needy. Otherwise we might leave the fulfilment of certain State duties—such as poor relief, in the widest sense of the words, is amongst others —like education and national defence with more right to share companies, only asking ourselves, Who will do it most cheaply? who will do it most effectively? If provision for the necessitous in a greater degree than is possible with the present poor relief legislation is a State duty, the State must take the matter in hand; it cannot rest content with the thought that a share company will undertake it."

The bill was referred to committee on March 21st, and it emerged into daylight again at the beginning of May. The Chancellor spoke on the second reading, proclaiming the workingman's "right to labour" (*Recht auf Arbeit*), as laid down in the common law of Prussia. He held that the State was ultimately responsible for the employment of those of its citizens who, through no fault of their own, lacked the opportunity to work, and thus the means of sustenance. It could not stand by and see them hunger. He cared not that this doctrine savoured of Socialism. "If an establishment employing twenty thousand or more workpeople were to be ruined . . . we could not allow these men to hunger. We should have to resort to real State Socialism and find work for them, and this is what we do in every case of distress. If the objection were right that we should shun State Socialism as we would an infectious disease, how do we come to organise works in one province and another in case of distress—works which we should not undertake if the labourers had employment and wages? In such cases we build railways whose profitableness is questionable ; we carry out improvements which otherwise would be left to private initiative. If that is Communism, I have no objection at all to it; though with such catchwords we really get no further." The measure was eventually passed by a substantial majority, and it became law of the land on July 6th, 1884. The Act was to come into operation on October 1st, 1885. Amendments and extensions were introduced in several later statutes, particularly those of May 28th, 1885 (which came into operation October 1st, 1885), extending insurance to the postal, telegraph, railway, naval and military administrative services, and to the carrying, inland navigation, and other trades ; May 5th, 1886 (in force since April 1st, 1888), extending insurance to workpeople engaged in agriculture and forestry ; March 5th, 1886, applying the law to civil service officials connected with the army and navy and to soldiers; July 11th, 1887 (in force since January 1st, 1888), affecting persons employed in building operations, and July 13th, 1887 (in force since January 1st, 1888), insuring sailors and all engaged in marine occupations.

Coming now to the provisions of the Sickness and Accident Insurance Laws, the two measures are made co-dependent, accident insurance being supplementary to sickness insurance, the period of incapacity determining when the one ends and the other begins. Speaking generally, these laws comprehend all the wages-earning classes, and it is estimated that they apply to over twelve million workpeople. Insurance is obligatory, save under certain circumstances in agriculture and forestry, for which there are special provisions. There can be no contracting out of either of the Acts, and the claims of the insured cannot be surrendered or renounced. Against sickness a labourer must insure himself in a Parochial or Local Sick Fund (*Gemeinde-* and *Ortskranken-kassen*), a Factory Sick Fund (*Fabrikkrankenkasse*), a Building Sick Fund (*Baukrankenkasse*), a Mining Sick Fund (*Knapp-schaftskasse*), a Guild Sick Fund (*Innungskasse*), or a Voluntary Relief Fund (*freie Hilfskasse*). As a rule the employer must pay one-third and the insured two-thirds of the premium, which is fixed at $1\frac{1}{2}$ to 2 per cent. of the average daily wages locally paid in the trade or industry of the insured, 3 per cent. being the maximum contribution. Relief is limited to thirteen weeks, after which the burden of maintenance is transferred to the local relief funds. The minimum relief consists of the provision of free medical treatment, medicine, bandages, and spectacles, if necessary, and in case the workman is incapacitated, sick money to the extent of half the wages earned by an ordinary day labourer in the place of his residence, this pay to date from the third day of his sickness. Instead of receiving this relief the sick man may be treated in hospital, though it must be with the consent of his family if he be married, or of his relatives if he be a member of a household. An important reservation is introduced in the case of the organised and free (as distinguished from parochial and local) relief societies. Here the sick money is fixed at half the average daily wages of the members of the society, the maximum being 3 or 4 marks, according to the two categories named in the law. Moreover, these societies afford women the same support for three weeks after confinement (in the case of agricultural and forest labourers, however, not in illegitimacy), and pay also funeral money equal to twenty times the daily wages earned in the deceased's trade. In the case of parochial sick funds the costs of administration come out of the rates, but other funds are self-supporting. An important characteristic of this measure is that it does not impose any formality upon workpeople in order to their insurance. They become *ipso facto* members of an insurance society because they work. The obligation to insure his workpeople lies with the employer, who pays the whole of the premiums in the first instance, but deducts the workpeople's share from their wages. Negligence or lax conduct on the part of employers is guarded against by penal provisions and by the strict control exercised by the supreme organ for the administration of the law.

Accident insurance begins after thirteen weeks of incapacity to work, owing to casualty. Compensation is recoverable for all accidents, even when occurring through negligence, with the single reservation that persons who wilfully injure themselves are excluded from benefit. The injured person is secured support and compensation, and in case of death his relatives, or those dependent upon him, receive compensation. Upon the employer rests the obligation to insure workpeople, and he does it at his entire cost, neither the insured nor the State assisting, as the Government originally proposed. For the purpose of insurance, the employers are organised into trade associations (*Berufsgenossenschaften*), with mutual liability, though special organisations exist for Imperial, State, and corporate undertakings. The premiums paid by the employers are fixed yearly upon the basis of (1) the amount of money paid in wages and salaries by the individual employer in the past year; and (2) the degree and character of risk incidental to his industry or trade, the latter provision requiring the creation of fixed categories or schedules of danger. The tariffs adopted by the trade associations receive the assent of the Imperial, or else of the State Insurance Office. As to compensation: in case of complete incapacity, the injured man receives during the period of his absence from work (beginning, as before stated, with the fourteenth week of his indisposition, the sickness insurance fund bearing the burden of his maintenance until then) two-thirds of his ordinary wages during the past year—the post-office being the medium of payment—and in case of partial incapacity, a portion of his usual wages, the amount depending upon his remaining earning capacity. The cost of medical attendance, after the first thirteen weeks of illness, is also borne by the insurance fund. In case of death, a sum equal to twenty times the deceased's daily earnings is given to the relatives instead of funeral money, the minimum amount being 30 marks (roughly £1 10s.), as well as an annuity to the same, payable at the end of every month, and fixed as follows: to a widow, until her death or re-marriage, one-fifth of her husband's earnings, for every child left 15/100 of his earnings until it attains the age of fifteen years, but one-fifth if the child has no mother. The combined annuities of a bereaved family cannot, however, exceed three-fifths of the father's earnings. In case the widow re-marries, she receives a final present equal to thrice her annuity. Should the deceased have been the support of relatives, as parents or grandparents, they, too, may be entitled to compensation, so long as the maximum of three-fifths of his earnings is not exceeded by the annuities granted.

It must be allowed that the liability thrown upon employers is very heavy, yet there is a compensating side in the great inducement which they feel to adopt precautionary measures against accident. The burden is also made lighter by the co-operative principle upon which the insurance societies are based. As to these a word or two. Private companies are entirely excluded from operating in this domain of industrial insurance. Employers are bound to organise themselves in trade associations, or the Federal Council may do the work for them. These associations (Gallicè *Associations des Professions*) may extend to the whole Empire, or only to a Federal State. They possess the right of self-government, though their statutes require the consent of the supreme Imperial (or State) Insurance Office. So far, the individual States have not cared to exercise the power which the law gives them (section 92) of establishing Central Insurance Offices for the control of the insurance associations formed within their territories, and the Imperial Insurance Office, or Board (*Reichsversicherungsamt*), in Berlin, has exercised universal jurisdiction with great advantage to the huge institution beneath its supervision. This authority must not be confounded with the "too bureaucratic" institution which Prince Bismarck in 1882 withdrew from his original scheme. The Imperial Insurance Office is a court of final instance in matters of organisation, administration, and discipline. Without trenching upon the functions entrusted to the Federal Council in regard to industrial insurance, it is responsible for the proper administration of the law. It is an organ subordinate to the Home Office, and it consists of at least three permanent and eight nonpermanent members. The president and the remaining permanent members are nominated by the Emperor on the recommendation of the Federal Council; of the other members, four are selected from the Federal Council, two are employers, and two represent insured workpeople. Another institution called into existence by the Accident Insurance Law is the Court of Arbitration (*Schiedsgericht*), whose duty it is to investigate accidents, and to fix the compensation to be paid.

IV. THE OLD AGE INSURANCE LAW.

The trio of insurance laws was completed in 1889 by the passing of a measure providing for the insurance of workpeople against the time of incapacity and old age (*Invaliditäts- und Altersversicherungsgesetz*). This was no after-thought suggested by the laws which preceded. It formed from the first part of the complete plan of insurance foreshadowed by Prince Bismarck over a decade ago, and in some of the Chancellor's early speeches on the social question he regarded the pensioning of old and incapacitated workpeople as at once desirable and inevitable. The speculation has been ventured that the Emperor Frederick, had he lived, might not, owing to his well-known political leanings, have been disposed to carry out this part of Bismarck's social programme.[1] It is, however, unlikely that any such departure from established policy would have been taken, unlikely even that it was meditated, for a draft law on the subject of old age insurance had been laid before the Reichstag before the death of the Emperor William. Whatever may have been the ideas of the Spring-time Emperor, his son, the present sovereign, early let it be understood, on his ascending the throne in the summer of 1888, that his social policy was that of the old Emperor and of Prince Bismarck. "It will be my en-

---

[1] Stress is laid upon the following passage in the rescript which the Emperor addressed to his Chancellor on March 12th, 1888 : "Sharing the views of my imperial father, I will warmly support all endeavours calculated to promote the economic prosperity of the various classes of society, to reconcile opposing interests in the same, and to ameliorate, as far as possible, inevitable evils; yet without creating the expectation that it is possible for State intervention to remove all social evils."

deavour," he said in his speech from the throne on June 25th,
"to carry on the work of imperial legislation in the sense in
which my late grandfather began it. I especially endorse to its
full extent the message issued by him on November 17th, 1881,
and in its sense I will continue to aim at legislation that will
give to the industrial population the protection which, in accordance with the principles of Christian ethics, it can afford to the
weak and the distressed in the struggle for existence." An
imperial utterance of November 22nd, 1888, was more pointed.
" As a valued legacy from my grandfather, I have undertaken
the task of carrying on the social-political legislation inaugurated
by him. I do not indulge the hope that the distress and misery
of mankind can be banished from the world by legislation, but I
regard it as the duty of the State to endeavour to ameliorate
existing economic evils to the extent of its power, and by means
of organic institutions to recognise, as a duty of the commonwealth, the active charity which springs from the soil of Christianity. The difficulties which attend the comprehensive insurance,
by State command, of workpeople against the dangers of age
and incapacity are great, but with God's help not insuperable."
Soon afterwards the Reichstag was called upon to consider this
final measure of insurance, and in June, 1889, it became law,
though it was left to the Emperor and the Federal Council to
determine the time of its coming into operation.

The Old Age Insurance Law is expected to apply to about
twelve million workpeople, including labourers, factory operatives,
journeymen, domestic servants, clerks, assistants, and apprentices
in handicrafts and in trade (apothecaries excluded), and smaller
officials (as on railways, etc.), so long as their wages do not reach
2,000 marks (about £100) a year; also persons employed in
shipping, whether maritime, river, or lake; and, if the Federal
Council so determine, certain classes of small independent undertakers. The obligation to insure begins with the completion of the
sixteenth year, but there are exemptions, including persons who,
owing to physical or mental weakness, are unable to earn fixed
minimum wages, and persons already entitled to public pensions,
equal in amount to the benefits secured by the law, or who are
assured accident annuities. The contributions are paid by the

employers and workpeople in equal shares, but the State also guarantees a yearly subsidy of 50 marks (£2 10s.) for every annuity paid. Contributions are only to be paid when the insured is in work. The law fixes four wages classes, with proportionate contributions, as follows :—

	Wages.		Contributions.		
			Weekly.	Yearly (47 weeks).	
1st class	300 marks	(£15)	14 pfennig	3·29 marks	(3s. 3½d.)
2nd ,,	500 ,,	(£25)	20 ,,	4·70 ,,	(4s. 8½d.)
3rd ,,	720 ,,	(£36)	24 ,,	5·64 ,,	(5s. 7½d.)
4th ,,	960 ,,	(£78)	30 ,,	7·05 ,,	(7s.)

Of course, of these contributions the workpeople only pay half. Old age annuities are first claimable at the beginning of the seventy-first year, but annuities on account of permanent incapacity may begin at any time after the workman has been insured for five years. The minimum period of contribution in the case of old age pensioning is thirty years of forty-seven premiums each. Where a workman is prevented by illness (exceeding a week but not exceeding a year), caused by no fault of his own, or by military duties, from continuing his contributions, the period of his absence from work is reckoned part of the contributory year. The annuities on account of incapacity are reckoned as follows. The sum of 60 marks (£3) is taken as a basis, and it is increased for every weekly contribution paid :—

In the first wages class (300 marks)	2 pfennig.
,, second ,, ,, (500 ,,)	6 ,,
,, third ,, ,, (720 ,,)	9 ,,
,, fourth ,, ,, (960 ,,)	13 ,,

Supposing, therefore, the insured person had contributed 1,800 weeks, of which 500 fell to the first class, 600 to the second, and 700 to the third, the annuity would be as follows :—

		Marks.
Basal annuity		60
500 × 2 pfennig	=	10
600 × 6 ,,	=	36
700 × 9 ,,	=	63
Imperial subsidy		50
		219 (nearly £11).

The annuity payable in the case of old age is reckoned at four pfennig for every contributory week in class 1, six in class 2, eight in class 3, and ten in class 4 of the wages classification. Here the number of contributory weeks is uniformly fixed at 1,410, but if a workman has paid premiums for more than that number of weeks while working in various wages classes, the annuity is calculated upon his 1,410 highest contributions.

Thus, supposing him to have contributed 400 weeks in class 1, 500 in class 2, 600 in class 3, and 900 in class 4, all the 900 contributions in class 4 and 510 of those in class 3 would be reckoned, and the annuity would therefore be :—

$$
\begin{array}{lll}
 & & \text{Marks.} \\
500 \text{ at } 8 \text{ pfennig} & = & 40\cdot80 \\
900 \text{ at } 10 \quad ,, & = & 90\cdot00 \\
\text{Imperial subsidy} & = & 50\cdot00 \\
\hline
 & & 180\cdot80 = (£9).
\end{array}
$$

The law contains many provisions intended to secure to workpeople equitable treatment during the first years of its operation, but it is impossible here to do more than indicate main outlines.[1] A few important stipulations must close this examination. An annuitant cannot claim both for old age and incapacity. Should an insured male who has contributed five years die before receiving an annuity, his widow (or in the event of her death the orphan children under fifteen years of age) is entitled to receive half the amount of his contributions. In case an insured female die under the same circumstances the claim may only be made on behalf of her children under fifteen years, if such exist. No such repayment of premiums can be made if the bereaved persons benefit under the Accident Insurance Law. Insurance is to take place in institutions established under the supervision of the Federal Council. Contributions are made in postage stamps affixed to yearly receipt cards supplied to the insured. Annuities are to be paid through the post-office monthly in advance, as in the case of accident assurance.

While these three measures of industrial insurance cannot but prove of enormous social value, it must not be forgotten that the

---

[1] For the sake of convenience the illustrations have been taken from an excellent text-book on the subject written by E. Pfafferoth, a German jurist of authority : "Führer durch die gesammte Arbeiter-versicherung" (Berlin : J. J. Heine, 1889).

great army of casual labourers and unemployed will receive no benefit. How can the position of this vast class be improved? To the problem here presented German statesmanship will no doubt seriously direct its attention before long. Prince Bismarck has avowed his recognition of the labourer's "right to work," a principle laid down in the common law of Prussia. His insurance laws seem, indeed, to demand the recognition of this "right" as a logical necessity. If the Chancellor will show the world how to solve the perplexing problem involved in the existence of a numerous class of labourers who are shut out from the employment which private enterprise is able to offer, he will further augment his already brilliant reputation as the first social reformer of the century.

CHAPTER X.

COMING to the domain of taxation we find not only that Prince Bismarck's theories have secured but partial realisation in law, but that his ideal comes far short of that set up by the scientific advocates of State Socialism. It is in the realm of finance that the Chancellor has suffered the most reverses. In no sphere of Parliamentary activity has he found the people with whom he has had to do conciliatory, not to say tractable, but here their perverseness has reached its climax. Wresting taxes from the Reichstag has, from the first, been like drawing water from flint. Many are the struggles which Prince Bismarck has had with incalcitrant Legislatures on the question of taxation. He has never been able to understand why Parliaments are so slow to recognise the necessity of taxes being levied for the meeting of national expenditure. More than once he has rebuked members of the Reichstag for having spoken of granting taxes to *him*, as if he needed them for himself. "I casually read or heard it said," he observed once, "'We have granted the Chancellor a hundred and thirty-five millions.' That is a curious expression. What do *I* want with the money? It is the same to me whether you grant money or not. But the expression 'grant' is false : you have resolved that the money shall be supplied for certain national purposes. If your decision was a proper one, you must stand by it ; if it was a wrong one, you should not have adopted it. But I have nothing to do with the money ; you do not grant money to me, but to the nation, the Empire : that is, you resolve that so and so much shall be employed for certain purposes, and without you we cannot expend it, but we do not owe you thanks for it all the same."

Sad experience has convinced him that an elected Legislature, dependent upon popular approbation for its existence, is as a rule a niggardly giver. When he had been but seven years Minister

President of Prussia he had to lament : "It is always unpleasant for a Government to need money, for those from whom it is required naturally do not give it readily, and have uses for their money which, if not better, are at any rate pleasanter to them than that of tax-paying. But a Government may say with Schiller : 'Does a cornfield grow upon my flat hand?'" He has learnt, too, that the most telling argument to place before the tax-payer is the pocket argument. "It is astonishingly easy," he philosophised once, "to say to the tax-payer, 'You pay too much'; and how ready to believe this is the man upon whom the taxes fall!"

I. DIRECT AND INDIRECT TAXATION.

Prince Bismarck declared in the Lower House of the Prussian Diet on January 15th, 1850, that "the burdens of the State should be borne by all citizens according to capacity." Holding this principle—at least in theory—it was inevitable that he would fall out with some of the direct imposts—including land, income, class,[1] building and trade taxes—which have so long been the basis of Prussian taxation. His views on the subject of direct *versus* indirect taxation deserve particular attention. It is not too much to say that the principle of taxation to which he holds most tenaciously is that of indirect taxation. He does not object—as we have seen—to raising part of the national revenue by direct taxes, but he holds that it is a sound financial principle to let indirect taxes contribute as large a proportion of the revenue as may be consistent with equality and the interests of the poor.

So early as 1851 Bismarck spoke in the Prussian Diet in favour of indirect as opposed to direct taxes. When a bill was submitted for the introduction of a new class and income tax, he opposed it (February 11th), and lauded the ancient corn and meat taxes [2]

---

[1] For the purposes of the class tax those liable are divided into classes according to degree of wealth, income, profession or trade, each class paying on a fixed scale.

[2] The corn and meat taxes (*Schlacht- und Mahlsteuer*) were taxes imposed on corn and meat entering certain towns. Since 1875 the corn tax has been totally repealed, but a local meat tax is still levied in a few places in Prussia. So lately as 1879 the Prussian Government endeavoured to re-introduce the latter tax as a communal tax, but the Diet did not share its sympathies. Prince Bismarck has never given these two taxes up as impossibilities.

which the new impost was intended to supplant. "I regard the corn and meat taxes," he said, "as the lightest and best of all the taxes we raise, and I regret that they have not been introduced in every town in the monarchy in place of the class tax. I am convinced that those towns which have replaced the corn tax by a class tax will in a few years desire this tax back again, and that the municipal authorities will see that it is impossible to raise direct taxes with an equivalent revenue. I cannot regard as very bad a tax which, like all indirect taxes, has in the course of several years, owing to its falling upon manifold contributors, produced an exact counterpoise, so that it is impossible to say with accuracy who bears it. . . . I have no hope of realising my wish for the universalisation of the corn and meat taxes, but I believe that when the towns which are no longer fortunate to possess these taxes have had a longer experience their populations will send us representatives holding very modified views on this subject."

Speaking on May 21st, 1869, in the Reichstag during the consideration of a Beer and Stock Exchange Tax Bill, he said :—

"The system to which these taxes belong is to me, at any rate, perfectly clear, and if they are elastic, so much the better, for so much greater will be the possibility of reaching the end I have in view. It is the natural end which everybody recognises as his own, that of so adjusting taxes that they may yield the same sum with the least pressure upon the tax-payers. The question arises then : Which taxes are these ? On the whole—at least for the unmonied classes of the people—they are not the direct taxes. A man with a net income of 100,000 thalers might under circumstances pay an income tax of 80 per cent., but some men cannot always scrape together their head-money, as it is called—the lowest schedule of the class tax. Thus I do not reckon direct taxes, which press on the tax-payer with a certain clumsy brutality—let him be monied or not—amongst the light taxes. Nor can I number amongst these the taxes upon the very necessaries of life, on bread and salt ; and if I were to allow myself to talk of the cruelty of embittering the poor man's pipe of tobacco or strengthening drink, and yet were conscious at the same time that I demanded head-money and bread tax for him, I should be honest enough to ask my inner self : ' What do you really mean by this hypocrisy ? '

So long as we tax bread, so long as we continue to demand the head-penny (*Kopfgroschen*) for every member of the labourer's family, and yet tax but slightly, or do not tax at all, the luxuries which I would allow to every one, even the poorest, but which, if he has no money, he must, for a time at least, do without, so long is the complaint about the corn and meat taxes and the head tax absolutely justified. The proper bases of a tax in the modern civilised State are, in my opinion, those articles of consumption which are used in sufficient quantity to yield a financial return exceeding the revenue from the so-called pure taxes on luxuries, which have so few objects of taxation that they scarcely pay the costs of control : they are the objects of luxury, if I may so call them, which are consumed wholesale, such as beer, brandy, wine, tobacco, tea, coffee, all articles from which one can for the moment abstain when his funds do not make them accessible. It is not desirable but it is possible to abstain from them. Much worse off is the man who has not paid his groschen of poll tax, and is as a consequence distrained, who has not paid his rent tax and is distrained for that, the man whose bread is made dearer by the corn tax—not so much owing to the height of the tax as the abuses in the increase of prices, for which the corn and meat taxes are sometimes made a pretext. The man cannot help himself: he must have bread ; beer is desirable, but if he cannot get it he is still able to exist."

The Chancellor cannot tolerate the idea that Germany, and Prussia in particular, should be so slow in accepting and applying the principle of indirect taxation. He told the Reichstag, February 22nd, 1878 :—

" In my opinion we are behind all great European States in regard to the development of our system of taxation, especially with respect to its reaction upon our economic conditions, and we have much ground to recover in this domain ; we have to ascertain how the great burdens which are caused by the extensive requirements of the Empire may be most easily borne, or, at any rate, how they may be borne more easily than now. I contend that at this moment every hundred million marks raised in England and France fall with less pressure on the population than with us."

When proposing the revision of the customs tariff in 1878, he declared that in making the Empire dependent upon customs and excise he was primarily influenced by the desire to extend the principle of indirect taxation, believing that such a mode of taxation caused the least hardship. In a letter addressed to the commission appointed to consider the tariff, and dated December 15th, 1878, he said:—

"The desideratum of financial reform takes with me the first place : the diminution of direct taxation by the increase of those of the Empire's revenues which are based on indirect taxes. . . . It is no accident that other great States, and especially those with far-advanced political and economic development, seek by preference to cover their expenditure by customs duties and indirect taxes. The direct tax—which is demanded of the individual taxpayer, is an amount fixed in advance for each single person liable, and in case of necessity is exacted from him by compulsion—falls, as from its nature it must do, with greater pressure than an indirect tax, the amount of which, both for the community and the individual, is determined by the consumption of the article taxed, and so far as the individual consumer is concerned is not as a rule paid by him separately, but in and with the price of the commodity bought. In the greater part of Germany the direct taxes, including the communal taxes, have reached a height which is oppressive, and economically does not appear justifiable. The greatest sufferers are the middle classes whose incomes range up to 6,000 marks, and who, owing to the direct taxes exacted by execution, or at any rate levied beyond their power to pay, find more often than the members of the lowest tax-schedules their economic stability undermined. If the reform in taxation is to give relief up to these limits—which I regard as necessary—it must begin with the revision of the customs tariff upon as wide a basis as possible. The more productive the customs tariff can be made financially, the greater will and must be the relief in the domain of direct taxation ; for it is self-evident that with the increase of the indirect revenues of the Empire an increase of the aggregate burden of taxation cannot be desired. The measure of this burden is not determined by the height of the revenues, but by the height of the requirements, by the height of the expenditure fixed by Government and Legislature as corresponding to the needs of the Empire or State. It can never be the intention of the Federal Governments to secure higher revenues than are absolutely necessary to the covering of these needs. They have only to strive to raise the requisite money in the way that is relatively easiest, and that is proved by experience to be the least oppressive. Thus every increase in the Empire's revenue from indirect taxes must carry with it the consequence that so much of the direct taxes, or of such indirect taxes as the State for special reasons no longer thinks it desirable to levy, will be remitted or assigned to communal unions as is not necessary to meeting the State expenditure fixed with the agreement of the Legislature. The financial reform to whose realisation the revision of the customs tariff should serve does not consist in the increase of the taxes necessary for the purposes of the Empire and the State, but in the commutation of the greater part of the unavoidable taxes into the less oppressive indirect taxes."

Prince Bismarck's views on indirect taxation were again on March 17th, 1881, laid before the Reichstag in the form of an address urging the importance of further developing this system of covering the Empire's financial needs. The address accompanied bills regulating the brewing tax, the imperial stamp tax, and introducing a tax upon young persons who did not, owing to physical and other reasons, undergo the usual period of military service. Certainly the yield of Germany in indirect taxes was not high at this time. A statement laid before the Reichstag showing the revenues of seven countries from customs duties, excise and stamp duties during 1879, put Germany in the lowest place :—

	Marks.	Per head of the population. Marks.
France	1,579,617,560	41·7
Great Britain and Ireland	1,090,205,438	36·7
United States	1,355,229,000	26·3
Italy	477,540,000	16·7
Austria . ·	365,382,600	16·4
Russia	1,205,095,400	14·1
Germany	467,409,028	10·4

The salt tax, which yields to the Empire some £2,000,000, Bismarck only defends on the ground of its necessity. Prior to

1867 salt was an article of State monopoly, but the *Zollverein* law
of October 12th, 1867, enacted : "The exclusive right of the
State to carry on trade in salt is so far as it now exists repealed,"
and a salt duty of six marks per cwt. net weight was introduced
instead, the re-established Empire retaining this duty when the
present imperial constitution was drawn up in 1871. Prince Bismarck said on May 1st, 1872, that he would be glad to abolish
the salt duty if only a substitute could be found. "My willing-
ness," he said, "to see it replaced by other sources of revenue is
as great as that expressed in the name of the Federal Governments,
only I must beg you not to persuade the Imperial Chancellor to
abandon assured imperial revenue, so long as he can help it, and
be thrown upon the more or less charitable contributions of the
individual States."

II. Exemption from Taxation.

Prince Bismarck would retain the income tax, but he would
follow the English system of exempting minimum incomes of a
considerable amount. He has spoken of a minimum of £300,
and even incomes of this amount should be placed in a low
schedule. For his idea is that earned income should be treated
leniently. On the other hand, income derived from the funds,
stocks, shares, and land should be taxed more freely. "He who
as a tradesman, a manufacturer, or an artisan earns an income by
daily work may run the risk of its diminution to-morrow," and he
is "unjustly taxed if he is expected to pay as much as the man
who has only to take a pair of scissors and clip coupons or to
write a receipt for the tenant who pays him rent." Again, he said
in the Prussian Lower House on February 4th, 1881 :—

" In regard to exemption from taxation, I hold in general the
principle that the man who has nothing but his two hands—that
is, untrained hands, which have learned no industry—wherewith
to earn his livelihood should be quite exempted from both State
taxes and communal contributions, and that the taxation should
begin when a further capital exists. This capital may take the
form of physical or mental skill, but it should in my opinion be
above the level of the simple artisan, who has not been able to
learn anything—though not from his own fault, but from the want

of means for his education. . . . He whose means are such that he has nothing in the world to rely upon but a varying ser-vice—as in Berlin the clearing away of snow in winter or digging in summer—should not be required by the State to do more than help in time of war to defend the common roof which protects him against the stranger. He should not be called on to pay money."

There is another class of people whom Prince Bismarck would exempt from national, though not communal, direct taxation, and that is the class of State officials. He argues that it is not only illogical but unjust to make State officials pay State taxes on State-paid income—an argument which, in a bureaucracy like Prussia, has an abundance of sympathisers. He represents the case as follows :—

" Either the official is adequately paid, or he is not adequately paid, or he is too highly paid. If he is too highly paid, a part of his salary may be taken from him ; if he is adequately paid, it is all right ; if he is not adequately paid, it is a very great hardship to curtail his salary by a tax." For the State to tax State-paid income is, he holds, like taxing its own coupons or its own debts.

Prince Bismarck is also opposed to the taxation of imperial revenue for communal purposes. On November 14th, 1874, a bill was introduced in the Reichstag legalising this exemption. Government action on the subject had been rendered necessary by the attempt made by the municipal authorities of Berlin to exact for the years 1867–1871 the sum of 468 marks (£23) on account of certain official buildings belonging to the Empire. The Chancellor was at once in arms, for he said that if the prin-ciple were admitted, from six to ten million marks might be de-manded. Speaking in favour of the bill on November 21st, he challenged the legal right of a commune to levy taxes of the kind, and speaking as the first officer of the Empire he said: " I cannot authorise the imperial treasury to pay one thaler which has not been sanctioned by you (the Reichstag) in the ordinary way of the Budget." At the same time he did not omit to pour con-tempt upon the people who were continually trying to "bore through the great imperial barrel." The measure did not pass owing to lack of time during that session.

III. EXCEPTIONAL TAXATION.

Early in his career Prince Bismarck was believed to be inclined to favour the land interest rather than the interest of industry in the matter of taxation. He complained in the Prussian United Diet, April 10th, 1848, that financial questions were contemplated "through the spectacles of industrialism rather than with the clear eye of the statesman, who surveys all the interests of the country with equal impartiality." While the rural districts were overburdened with taxation, the towns came off too easily. For this reason he opposed the abolition of taxes like the corn and meat taxes, which benefited the country at the expense of the town. In later years, however, he has shown no desire to give to the land interest any preference. He would make the land bear a liberal share of the country's burdens, but with the proviso that invested capital should at least be placed in the same category with landed property so far as concerns taxation. He has never been opposed to an income tax, and a high one, so long as small incomes were exempted. When debating a measure on the subject in the Prussian Lower House in 1850, he said : "Section 6 of the bill fixes the percentage of the income tax at 3. I should have been glad if it had been higher, and I believe that with a proper distinction between such income as is derived from property and such as is based on personal service a higher tax might have been imposed without causing hardship."

On February 18th, 1850, he spoke as follows of the taxation of invested capital : "I do not understand why the man who derives his income from land—perhaps with great personal exertion and great risk, since he must under all circumstances and in all conjunctures be prepared to meet his creditors—should be taxed so much higher than the man who puts money into his pocket quite easily by coupon-clipping or by collecting interest on mortgages."

Over thirty years later he said the same thing (June 14th, 1882) : "It is quite natural that we may have to fall back on a higher tax on invested capital, and in the lack of other resources we shall have to do so ; for the only direct tax which we can still impose is a tax on funded income, which is acquired merely by coupon-clipping, and one higher than the uncertain income which is earned by mental, manual, and pen work, or by capital at the expense of danger and risk."

IV. PRINCE BISMARCK AS A FISCAL REFORMER.

It was, however, after the re-establishment of the Empire that Prince Bismarck first came forward as a great fiscal reformer. In 1875 he undertook the gigantic work of remodelling the imperial taxation of Germany. To this undertaking he was driven by financial necessity. When it was sent into the world clothed in a new and improved constitution the Empire received a hand-some portion in the form of fixed sources of revenue, these including customs and excise, posts, telegraphs, and Alsace-Lorraine railways, bill stamps, etc. Article 35 of the imperial constitution provides :—

" The Empire shall have the exclusive right to legislate concerning everything that relates to the customs ; the taxation of salt and tobacco manufactured or raised in the territory of the Confederation ; the taxation of manufactured brandy and beer, and of sugar and syrup prepared from beets or other native productions ; also to legislate concerning the mutual protection of taxes upon articles of consumption levied in the several States of the Empire ; against embezzlement ; as well as concerning the measures necessary in granting exemption from the payment of duties for the security of the common customs frontier. In Bavaria, Wurtemberg, and Baden the taxation of home brandy and beer is reserved to the State Legislature. The Federal States shall, however, endeavour to effect uniform legislation regarding the taxation of these articles."

Article 38 says :—

" The revenue accruing from the duties and other imposts mentioned in article 35, from the latter so far as they are subject to imperial legislation, shall go to the imperial treasury " [after deduction of costs of collection, etc.].

Article 49 says :—

" The revenues from the post and telegraph system shall be for the entire Empire in common. The expenses shall be paid

out of the common receipts, and the surplus shall go to the
Imperial Treasury."

But the new Empire soon fell into extravagant ways, and its
fortune proved insufficient. The revenues ensured to it did not
cover the current expenditure, the deficit being made up by the
various States, which contributed in proportion to population.
These "matricular contributions" grew in time to an extent that
pointed to the necessity for increasing the Empire's own independent resources. As a matter of fact, the Chancellor had
never liked the "matricular" system, which in his eyes was an
indignity to the Empire, and he refused to regard it as a permanent
institution. As early as 1872 he had told the Reichstag, "An
Empire founded on the theory of matricular contributions lacks
the strong bond of cohesion which is furnished by a common
system of finance." Hitherto Prince Bismarck had but dabbled
in financial reforms. He had, it is true, introduced a new imperial currency and the gold standard,[1] and had made the Imperial
Bank out of the old Prussian Bank, but the higher regions of
finance had hardly been entered. When, however, the Imperial
Treasury had fallen into chronic decline the Chancellor thought
it time to take in hand the question of taxation. In 1875 it was
anticipated that the ordinary revenues of the Empire would leave
a deficit of 87 million marks, the income being estimated at
$312\frac{1}{2}$ millions and the expenditure at $399\frac{1}{2}$ millions. The usual
amount of the matricular contributions had been about 70 millions,
but now the highest call ever made upon the Federal States
would have to be greatly exceeded if this system of imperial relief
were adhered to. The occasion seemed a favourable one for
reviving the general question of matricular contributions, and
Prince Bismarck made a bold attempt to get rid of them once
for all.

Addressing the Reichstag on November 22nd, 1875, he said :—

" A thorough reform in taxation, including a customs reform—
who does not wish it ! But it is a Herculean task, which one must

---

[1] Upon the question of the standard the German Government has evidently
not made up its mind finally.   If England adopted the double standard, so
would Germany.

have by way of experiment approached in the capacity of a comparative layman, such as I am, in order properly to comprehend its difficulty. With one pull at this net, under which we are now caught as regards taxation, all the meshes clink into the smallest States ; each State has its particular wishes. A thorough-going reform cannot be carried out without the willing, active, helpful co-operation of every individual Government with the Empire. For I cannot regard it as a reform merely to impose new imperial taxes without abolishing old ones. . . . The individual Federal Governments must, in a reform, remove as many taxes as they save in matricular contributions ; the means of doing this, however, are not possessed by the Reichstag but by the various Diets. Only when we lighten the matricular contributions does it become the task of the Diets to erect battering trains against their Ministries, so as to make them alleviate the most oppressive taxes in a corresponding degree. . . . I do not know whether my ideas of reform in taxation find general approval ; but even if they do not, I shall not be restrained from following my convictions and waiting to see in what way it will be possible to commend them to the legislative bodies. Speaking entirely from the standpoint of the Empire, I seek as great a diminution as possible, if not the complete abolition, of the matricular contributions. It is scarcely disputed that the form of these contributions is such that they do not fall on the contributing States according to their capacity to contribute. I might call it a rough form, which may serve as a makeshift so long as it is impossible to furnish the Empire in its early youth with revenues of its own. If, however, it be acknowledged that this form of taxation does not act justly, it cannot, judged from my political standpoint as Imperial Chancellor, be a means of consolidating the Empire. The feeling of being called on to perform unjust services encourages the endeavour after freedom from such injustice."

This speech was made incidental to the endeavour of the Government to pass bills increasing the beer tax and introducing a tax on Stock Exchange transactions (*Börsensteuer*). These proposals, however, made no headway. Neither by reasoning with the Reichstag nor by offering it uncommon deference did the Chancellor achieve any result. " I fully agree," he said,

" that in no domain of State affairs is the decision of the Reichstag as a final court of appeal more unquestionable than in that of
questions of taxation, in that of determining the mode in which
we shall raise the revenues required for the State both in the
Empire and in the individual States.   You are in a position—I
might say—to act with the forbearance of omnipotence and *sine
ire et studio* to judge the question entirely from the standpoint :
Is it expedient that the revenues required by the Government
should in part be raised in the way proposed or not?   If a
Government did not unconditionally respect the rights of a Legislature in questions of finance—even as to matters of form—con-
stitutionalism would not have made a beginning.   Be at rest in
this respect, and be conciliatory in the knowledge of your strength,
which in this domain is unassailable."

But it was no good : the Reichstag heard the Chancellor's
flattering words with astonished satisfaction, but nevertheless said
" Nay " to his pressing request for more taxes.   Still, the idea of
financial reform was not abandoned.   Bismarck only waited for a
more convenient season in which to approach Parliament again.
This did not come until 1878, after ministerial changes had made
his way clearer.   The imperial speech opening the Reichstag on
February 6th of that year said : " The Federal Governments do
not think it advisable to meet the Empire's need of larger resources by increasing the contributions of the various States.
The general financial position of Germany points rather to the
augmentation of the Empire's own revenues.   For this purpose
a bill will be laid before you for the levying of imperial stamp
duties and the taxation of tobacco."   In this way it was hoped to
render the Empire independent of the objectionable matricular
contributions.   He remarked, indeed, on February 26th :—

" You know from my own mouth that I am an opponent of
direct and a friend of indirect taxes, and that in this domain I
am striving after a comprehensive reform which will make the
Empire really rich, instead of being poor as now.   My ideal is not
an Empire which must collect its matricular contributions at the
doors of the individual States, but an Empire which, having in its
hands the principal source of good finance, indirect taxes, would
be in a position to pay contributions to all the individual States."

For the ten months preceding the convocation of the Reichstag Prince Bismarck had lived in nominal retirement at Varzin, but he returned to active office after a conference with the leader of the National Liberal party had convinced him that the Conservatives would in the new Parliament have a valuable ally, with whose assistance the Government might hope to carry through its immediate schemes. During the debate on the tobacco bill Prince Bismarck admitted (February 26th) that his ideal was a State monopoly of the tobacco trade, and that the measure before the House was merely transitional. Perhaps because alarmed at this frank statement, the Reichstag shook its head at the two proposals, one of which it shelved by referring it to a committee charged with the duty of comprehensive inquiries. An election was hastened by an attempt on the Emperor's life, and the financial measures were lost sight of for a time. The attention of the Legislature was temporarily turned into new channels, but a drastic Socialist law having been passed, the Chancellor was able to return to the question of finance. Now began the real era of economic reform, the first step in which was the revision of the customs tariff—referred to already—a measure completed on July 9th, 1879, the new tariff becoming law on July 15th. The agreement arrived at between the Reichstag and the Government was facilitated by the adoption by the latter of what is known as the Frankenstein clause. During the consideration of the tariff, the fear was expressed on many sides that if the Government were made independent of the matricular contributions it would pass from the control and influence of the Reichstag. Hence "constitutional guarantees" were asked for. Prince Bismarck did not think any were needed, yet he had no difficulty in accepting the compromise proposed June 20th, 1879, by the late Baron von Frankenstein, a Clerical deputy, which was that when the revenue from the customs and tobacco duty exceeded 120,000,000 marks, the excess should be transferred by the Empire to the various States, being divided in proportion to population.[1]

---

[1] From this provision proceeded the well-known Prussian "lex Huene," by which a certain portion of the sum accruing to Prussia from the imperial customs revenue is not to be applied to State purposes, but to the reduction of the land and building taxes levied locally, and to other communal purposes.

V. LATER FISCAL PROPOSALS.

Since 1879 Prince Bismarck has made many other attempts to develop his great scheme of fiscal reform. His monopoly projects have been dealt with separately. Other measures have been a Stamp (Bourse) Tax Law, passed June 13th, 1881—introduced four times in ten years—then estimated to make Stock Exchange transactions contribute 20,000,000 marks to the imperial treasury; and Brandy and Sugar Taxation Laws. In the promotion of all these measures the idea of converting direct into indirect taxes has always exercised equal influence with the desire to improve the Empire's finances. It must be confessed, however, that Prince Bismarck has had more failures than successes with his financial proposals. In 1881 he asked the Reichstag to accept a measure for the taxation of young men who were exempted from military service from physical unfitness and other reasons. The *Begrün-dung* stated that the number of exemptions was very great, and thus the burden of military service fell unequally. If, however, citizens could not do duty in the army, they could pay for the support of those who did. Similar laws existed already in Bavaria and Wurtemberg, as well as Austria and Switzerland. It was expected that the tax would yield some millions of marks. This proposal did not commend itself to the Reichstag, which rejected it on May 7th, 1881.

The idea of an imperial income tax, apart from the income tax levied by the individual States, was first broached in the Reichstag in 1872, when (June 3rd) a private proposal was introduced for the taxing of public companies as an initial measure. It was stated that the great Berlin lending bank, the *Discontogesellschaft*, had during the preceding year made profits of 5,000,000 marks (roughly £246,000), giving a dividend of 25 per cent. Why, it was asked, should this great concern pay the Empire no taxes, while the Vienna *Creditanstalt*, with about the same profits, paid the Austrian Government 914,000 gulden. Prince Bismarck did not, however, at this time take the hint, though on March 10th, 1877, he threatened that he would resort to an imperial income tax unless the Reichstag found him other sources of revenue. Quite recently the Radical party proposed the introduction of such a tax, to be levied on net income from funded capital, landed property, trade and business, public or private employment bringing profit, *rente*, or other income, but incomes below 6,000 marks (roughly £300) were to be exempted. The tax was to be progressive, rising by ½ per cent. stages. The Radicals, however, only secured the support of the Social Democrats for this proposal.

Prince Bismarck made a bold attack on the *laissez-faire* principle when he passed the Usury Law of 1880. This law was particularly intended to prevent the plundering of small landowners and artisans by the predatory part of the money-lending community. The Diets of Prussia, Bavaria, and Hesse-Darmstadt had all deliberated upon the question before imperial action was taken. In 1879 an interpellation addressed to the Federal Government excited discussion on the subject, and the necessity of legislation was pretty generally recognised. Private bills were this year promoted for the punishment of illegitimate money-lending, and these bills were referred to committee, but without any definite result. During a Reichstag debate in 1879 a Conservative deputy went so far as to propose the introduction of legal rates of interest, viz., 6 per cent. for trade and 5 per cent. for other loans, though 8 per cent. was to be allowed in exceptional cases. This proposal did not, however, receive encouragement. On April 8th, 1880, a Usury Law was introduced in the form of additions to the Imperial Penal Code. This provided that : " Whosoever shall take advantage of the distress, indiscretion, or inexperience of another, and persuade him to promise or give to himself or a third party interest upon a loan which so exceeds the usual interest as to be flagrantly disproportionate to the service rendered, may be punished for extortion with imprisonment for a period not exceeding six months, simultaneous fine up to 3,000 marks (roughly £150), and eventually with loss of civil rights. . . . Whosoever practises such extortion as a business may be punished with imprisonment for a period not less than three months, and a fine varying from 150 to 15,000 marks (£7 10s. to £750), with the loss of civil rights. . . . Contracts contravening the provisions of this law are declared to be null and void." This measure received the final consent of the Reichstag on May 7th, and it became law soon afterwards. The Conservatives and Clericals supported the Government, and the National Liberals and Radicals were found in opposition.

Naturally enough there have been times when Prince Bismarck and the Reichstag have both acted illogically upon the subject of State Socialism. The Chancellor, for instance, refuses to have anything to do with the payment of members principle which the Reichstag affirmed so early as February, 1874. Its advocates contend that payment of members is a reasonable conclusion to draw from the axioms to which Prince Bismarck has accustomed Parliament, while he, for his part, believes the payment system to be inexpedient and injurious to Parliamentary life. On the other hand, the Postmaster-General was in 1885 unable to pass a democratic measure like his Postal Savings Bank Law, the object of which, avowed and actual, was to promote thrift amongst the working classes. The Radicals objected that it was another measure of State Socialism, the capitalists opposed it because it was likely to injure existing savings banks, and between the two fires the bill fell. It will be clear from what has been said in the preceding pages that fiscal reform constitutes an unfinished chapter in the history of Prince Bismarck's economic legislation.

CHAPTER XI.

IT remains now to indicate the positive measures which have been taken during the State Socialistic era to further the commercial interests of Germany abroad. One of the motives for the introduction of import duties was the protection of home trade. Foreign trade has been encouraged by the establishment of an efficient consular system, by the conclusion of favourable commercial treaties with countries offering receptive markets, and by colonisation. Perhaps no country takes so practical a view of consular functions as Germany, whose consular agents abroad are expected to aid the extension of German trade to the best of their power. The consuls are, to begin with, recommended to the Emperor for appointment by the committee of the Federal Council to which commercial questions are committed, and the law regulating the consular system says expressly that it is the duty of these officials " to protect and to promote the interests of the Empire, especially in regard to trade, commerce, and navigation, as far as possible." A considerable number of the imperial consuls belong to the category *Berufs-consul (consul missus)*, having received legal, politico-economical, and technical training for their duties. It is safe to say that such an anomaly as a sinecure is unknown in the German diplomatic and consular service. Even ambassadors do not regard it as derogatory—and why should they ?—to keep their eyes open to the commercial interests of their country. It was for the better qualification of its representatives in the East that an Oriental Seminary was established at State cost in connection with the Berlin University in 1887. Here Turkish, Arabic, Persian, Japanese, Chinese, and other Eastern languages are taught to students intending to follow a diplomatic or consular

career. The resources of the Empire have been placed at the
service of foreign commerce in a multitude of other ways, one
way being the support of manufacturers participating in international exhibitions, beginning with the Philadelphia and Sydney
exhibitions of 1876 and 1879 respectively.

But the most remarkable illustration of State intervention on
behalf of industry and trade is furnished by Prince Bismarck's
active promotion of colonial enterprise.[1] It can hardly be said
that the Chancellor here inaugurated an entirely new departure
in German politics, for, long ago though the incident took place,
Brandenburg had in the days of the Great Elector Frederick
William secured a footing in Africa. In 1681 this gallant Hohen-
zollern established a trading colony on the Gold Coast, and in
1686 made acquisitions north of Senegal, nor would his colonial
enterprises have been limited to Africa if death had not removed
him in 1688, for he had purposed colonisation in America. The
Great Elector's son, Frederick I. of Prussia, preserved the foreign
possessions thus secured, but Brandenburg's (now Prussia's)
colonial schemes received no encouragement from King Frederick
William I., who, preferring the material equivalent of his transoceanic territories to the barren dignity of colonial empire, placed
his colonies in Guinea in the market at the sum of 150,000
thalers. No purchaser could be found at the price, and ultimately (in 1720) a Dutch trading company became the possessor
for 7,200 ducats and twelve Moors, of whom six bore gold chains
about their necks.   In 1871 Great Britain acquired Prussia's
old Gold Coast colony by purchase, and it is now an appendage
of Cape Coast Castle.   Arguin, north of Senegal, was captured
by the French about the same time that Frederick William I.
sold his more southern possessions. From that time down to
the re-establishment of the Empire, Prussia kept clear of colonial
enterprises, which, indeed, had brought her no glory.

Whether the inauguration of a colonial policy, whether the
elevation of Germany to the position of a Colonial Power—not

---

[1] " Deutsche Colonialgeschichte," in two vols., by Max von Koschitzky
(Leipzig : Baldamus, 1888), is an excellent and comprehensive work on this
subject.

yet, indeed, of high *prestige*—can be numbered amongst Prince Bismarck's acts of real statesmanship, is a question which the future will determine. It is far too soon to judge of the colonial developments of German foreign policy. All that can be said is that a beginning has been made in the building up of an empire beyond the seas, and that national honour, if not national interest, requires that, the hand having been put to the plough, there shall be no looking back. To use the words of an authoritative writer on the subject, " the colonial movement has *nolens volens* become an affair of honour with Germany. . . . The retrogression which some of her friends both at home and abroad so much desire is no longer possible. The motto of every patriotic German is ' Forward ! ' " [1] The position could not be better stated.

A host of theoretical reasons are often advanced for Germany's colonial departure, but as a matter of fact it was dictated by practical considerations alone, and by few of these. It is not at all a matter of over-population at home or of diverting the tide of emigration into new channels, but simply and solely of trade, new markets, and gold. Probably two millions of Germans have left their country for ever during the last thirty years, but Prince Bismarck did not decide to encourage the acquisition of colonies in order to establish either Greater or Less Germanies across the seas.[2] It is now allowed that in none of the many colonies which have during the last six years been placed under German protection is the climate such as Europeans can tolerate. The Chancellor's colonial policy is but a practical endorsement of the old axiom that " Trade follows the flag." Germany's colonies are intended to offer new markets for her developing industries.

The colonial policy of Prince Bismarck is generally regarded as having been inaugurated when the Chancellor on April 24th, 1884, telegraphed to the German Consul at Capetown authority to immediately place the possessions of Herr F. A. Lüderitz, a Bremen merchant, in South-west Africa—by name Angra Pequena—

---

[1] Johannes Baumgarten in " Die deutschen Kolonien und die nationalen Interessen," pp. 8, 9. (Cologne, 1885.)
[2] See Appendix E for Prince Bismarck's views on emigration.

under the protection of the Empire.   But the colonial idea was
in the air long before that.   It derived a certain prominence in
1880, when the Imperial Government proposed to afford the
Deutsche Seehandlungsgesellschaft, a company engaged in foreign
trade, financial assistance, in order to enable it the better to maintain its prestige in the South Seas, especially in the Samoan
Islands.   This company intended, helped by imperial gold, to
take over the lands and plantations owned in the South Seas by
a Hamburg firm, and the Reichstag was asked to empower the
Chancellor to guarantee the shareholders $4\frac{1}{2}$ per cent. interest on
their investments for twenty years, if necessary, the subsidy not,
however, exceeding 3 per cent. of the paid-up capital.   This proposal was promptly rejected, and the Government made no further
attempt to gain for it the Reichstag's favour.   Speaking on December 1st, 1884, Prince Bismarck said that his Parliamentary
defeat on this question damped his colonial ardour, and it was
only when, four years later, he believed that the country was with
him that he again ventured to take up the colonial question.

While Germany laid the foundation of a colonial empire by the
acquisition in 1884 of South-west African territory, she had already
put out feelers in West Africa the year before.   In the summer
of 1882, Great Britain and France concluded a convention delimit-
ing and restricting their respective spheres of influence on the
West Coast.   Other countries were taking stock of their interests
in West Africa, and Germany, not desiring to suffer disadvantage,
followed the example.   In a circular letter of April, 1883, the
Foreign Office asked the Senates of the Hanse Towns to state
their wishes and possible complaints regarding trade and navigation in that part of the world.   At this time Hamburg firms
were established in Sierra Leone, Liberia (Monrovia, Grand Bassa,
Sinoe, and Cape Palmas), the Gold Coast, Accra, Wydah, Little
and Great Popo, Porto Novo, Lagos, Cameroon, and the coast of
Biafra, Gaboon and the neighbourhood, Ambriz and Kinsembo.
Bremen firms were also established at many points of the West
Coast, and the North German and Basel Missionary Societies had
stations in various places.   The Senate of Hamburg readily acknowledged the fair treatment and willing protection granted by
the British authorities to Germans resident in British colonies and

settlements, but did not conceal the disadvantages under which German trade was carried on in the absence of German rights of suzerainty and therefore of interference on the African coast. It therefore urged the Government to acquire a naval station and a piece of coast-land on the West Coast for the establishment of a trading colony, a recommendation which the Hamburg Chamber of Commerce supported.

The Government at once decided to appoint a commissioner for the care of German commercial interests in West Africa, and to station ships of war on the coast. Dr. Gustav Nachtigal was the official sent out, and his instructions, as contained in a letter of May 19th, 1884, were to secure a preponderance of influence for Germany in Angra Pequena, the coast between the Niger delta and Gaboon, in the Cameroon region, and Little Popo. Dr. Nachtigal soon proved himself a zealous colonist, hoisting his flag at some points—as at Benita—where, according to his own reports sent home, other countries evidently had prior rights. The permanent acquisitions of the year 1884 were Angra Pequena (with Great Nama Land and Damara Land), Togo Land, Cameroon, some East African territories, and part of New Guinea. Angra Pequena was annexed contrary to the wish of the Cape Government, and dilatoriness on the part of the Colonial Office in London was alone responsible for the loss of this territory to the British Crown. It was only after the German Foreign Office had for many months vainly urged Lord Granville to state whether or not England laid claim to the country, that Prince Bismarck gave instructions for the hoisting of the German flag at various points on the coast from Cape Frio in the north to the Orange River in the south, the British possession of Walfisch Bay being, of course, excluded.

At this time a veritable colonial fever infected the people of Germany, and the newspapers wrote about little else than the expansion of the Empire. Speaking in the Reichstag on June 26th, 1884, Prince Bismarck explained the Government's attitude in the following plain words :—

"As regards the colonial question in the narrower sense of the words, I will explain its genesis. We were first induced, owing to the enterprise of the Hanseatic people—beginning with land purchases and leading to requests for imperial protection—to consider whether we could promise protection to the extent desired. I have not abandoned my former aversion to colonies—I will not say colonies after the system mostly adopted last century, the French system, as it might now be called—but colonies which make a strip of land their foundation, and then seek to draw emigrants, appoint officials, and establish garrisons. This mode of colonisation may be good for other countries, but it is not practicable for us. I do not believe that colonial projects can be artificially established, and all the examples which Deputy Bamberger advanced as warnings in committee were cases in which the wrong way had been taken : where people had wished to construct harbours where there was no traffic, and build towns where there were no people, the intention being to attract people by artificial means to the place. Very different is the question whether it is expedient, and whether it is the duty of the German Empire, to grant imperial protection and a certain amount of support in their colonial endeavours to those of its subjects who devote themselves to such undertakings relying upon the protection of the Empire, in order that security may be ensured in foreign lands to the communities which grow naturally out of the superfluous strength of the German body politic. This question I answer affirmatively : I certainly do so less reservedly from the standpoint of expediency, though from the standpoint of the State's duty I do so unconditionally. . . .

" My intention, as approved by the Emperor, is to leave the responsibility for the material development of a colony, as well as its inauguration, to the action and the enterprise of our seafaring and trading citizens, and to proceed less on the system of annexing the transoceanic provinces to the German Empire than that of granting charters, after the form of the English Royal Charters, encouraged by the glorious career which the English merchants experienced in the foundation of the East India Company ; also to leave to the persons interested in the colony the government of the same, only granting them European jurisdiction for Europeans and so much protection as we may be able to afford without maintaining garrisons. I think, too, that a colony of this kind should possess a representative of the Imperial Authority with the title of Consul or Resident, whose duty it would be to receive complaints ; while the disputes which might arise out of these commercial enterprises would be decided by one of our Maritime or Mercantile Courts at Bremen, Hamburg, or somewhere else. It is not our intention to found provinces but commercial under-takings."

In January, 1885, the Chancellor could say that " the colonial movement has been in flux for two years, and the reception given to it has far surpassed my expectations." He complained, how-ever, that the Reichstag handicapped him seriously, for there the Radicals disputed every proposal of the Government for the strengthening and the extension of the young colonial empire. Early in the year he threatened to abandon his colonial policy unless the hostile attitude of the Reichstag were modified. There had been a sanguinary conflict between the German marines and the natives in Cameroon in December, 1884, and the Radicals made this untoward incident and the appearance of strained relations with Great Britain at the time a pretext for renewed opposition. Speaking on January 10th, 1885, the Chancellor denied that there was any likelihood of a quarrel with this country either then or at any time, and he used these noteworthy words :—

" I absolutely dispute this possibility ; it does not exist, and all the questions which are now a subject of dispute between us and England are not important enough to justify a breach of the peace between us either over there or on our part in the North Sea, and I do not know what other disputes can arise between us and England ; there have never yet been any. So far as I can remember we have only once in our history been at war with England ; that was in the years 1805 and 1806. I will not refer to details here, but the situation was a completely unnatural one, for the Prussia of that day was coerced by the overbearing France. So far as my diplomatic experience goes, I can conceive of no cause that could possibly lead to hostility between us and England ; an inconceivable English Ministry, such as neither exists now, nor, judging by the hereditary political wisdom of the English nation, is probable, would have to attack us in the most wanton manner—then, my God, we would defend ourselves !— but, apart from this improbability, there is no reason for a breach of the peace, and I regret that the previous speaker has, through his allusions, compelled me even to express my conviction that it is not possible. Our differences of opinion regarding England will never within conceivable time be of such moment that they cannot be removed by honourable good-will and discreet and cautious diplomacy, such as will certainly be exhibited on our side."

In 1885 further stimulus was given to the colonial movement by the passing of a law empowering the Government to subsidise mail steamship lines to East Asia and Australia for a period of fifteen years to the extent of £200,000 a year. This measure was foreshadowed as early as 1881, but a definite legislative proposal on the subject had to be rejected once by the Reichstag before it could succeed. Prince Bismarck fought for the measure with characteristic energy. "Without subsidised steamers I have no prospect of carrying on a colonial policy," he declared on March 13th, 1885, on which account he originally proposed that the State-supported lines should provide communication between West and East Africa and the home country. Africa was, however, crossed out of the bill, and the Chancellor submitted, with the philosophic remark, " We must take what we can get."

Nearly all Germany's colonial acquisitions were secured in the years 1884 and 1885, and those which succeeded Angra Pequena, Cameroon, and Togo Land may now be enumerated. A beginning in colonisation was made in East Africa the former year. The Society for German Colonisation sent an expedition out, under the direction of Dr. Karl Peters, with the result that in November and December of 1884 the territories of Useguha, Nguru, Usagara, and Ukami, coast-lands lying opposite Zanzibar, were acquired by treaty with the chiefs. Letters of protection were granted the following year to the company, which now took the name of German East African Company, and entered upon a series of important extensions of territory, including Somali Land to the north. The establishment of German influence in East Africa was not secured without serious trouble with the Sultan of Zanzibar, and at one time warlike measures were contemplated by Germany. Towards the close of 1886 Great Britain and Germany arrived at an agreement intended to secure the rights of the Sultan and to determine the respective spheres of influence of the two European Powers in East Africa. This, however, did not prevent the Company from falling out with the Zanzibar potentate for a second time in 1888, when serious outbreaks occurred in the interior, fomented, it is alleged, by the Sultan. As a consequence the Company's territories became disorganised, and a large part of the work of subjugation and civilisation already achieved was undone. Dr. Peters, the Company's pioneer and virtual founder, conducted an expedition in 1889 from the Zanzibar coast into the interior in search of Emin Pasha, and the report of his death reached Europe at the end of the year, though its truth has not yet been confirmed. In 1885 Germany's influence in East Africa was extended by another company of capitalists who acquired Vitu (Suaheli Land), an equatorial territory, which was forthwith placed under imperial protection. With this country Germany, or rather Prussia, had had relations since 1867.

It was likewise in 1884 that colonisation really began in New Guinea. In that year the territories of the " German Trading and Plantation Company " and of a Hamburg firm of merchants in that island passed into the hands of the New Guinea Company, to which letters of protection were granted in 1885. In April of the latter year a treaty was concluded between Great Britain and Germany determining the respective spheres of influence of the two countries in New Guinea. The island is now divided amongst three States. Great Britain possesses the southern portion, opposite Australia ; Germany the northern portion (called Kaiser Wilhelmsland) and the Bismarck Archipelago (New Britain Archipelago) ; and Holland the western portion. The possessions of the New Guinea Company, which in 1887 drew the Solomon Islands within its net, extend to more than half the area of the German Empire. By treaty of April 6th, 1886, the limits of the German and British spheres of influence in the Western Pacific— " for the purpose of this declaration," runs the agreement, " the expression Western Pacific means that part of the Pacific Ocean lying between the 15th parallel of north latitude and the 30th parallel of south latitude and between the 165th meridian of longitude west and the 130th meridian of longitude east of Greenwich "—have been carefully defined.

In the summer of 1885 the Caroline Islands, lying north of
New Guinea, were placed under German protection; but Spain at
once vigorously protested, and on the dispute being referred to
the Pope, she was found to have prior rights, and the annexation
was consequently renounced.   As recompense, Germany the
same year took the unclaimed Marshal Islands, likewise in the
South Seas, so far the smallest territory placed under German
protection, a territory whose trade had for many years been in
German hands.

The last edition of " Perthes' Atlas " (1889) gives the following table of Germany's colonies :—

Africa:	Square kilometres.	Population.		
Togo	1,300	40,000		
Cameroon	40,000	480,000		
Damara and Nama Land . .	650,000	150,000		
Usagara, Useguha, etc. (East Africa)	61,000	750,000		
Vitu	1,200	15,000		
		753,500		1,435,000
Oceania:				
Kaiser Wilhelmsland . . .	181,650	110,000		
Bismarck Archipelago . . .	47,100	190,000		
Marshal Islands	400	11,000		
		229,150		311,000
Totals . . .	982,650	1,746,000		

So far as it is possible to judge, the measures taken to establish
for Germany a colonial empire do not offer brilliant prospects,
but the ultimate results will naturally depend in great measure
upon the foresight displayed and the discretion exercised by
those private individuals upon whom depends the development
of most of Germany's transoceanic acquisitions.   With three
exceptions—Cameroon, Angra Pequena, and Togo, which are
administered as Crown colonies—these territories are left to
private enterprise, though full imperial protection is guaranteed.
It is significant, however, that Prince Bismarck has already been
compelled by stress of circumstances to intervene to a far greater
extent than he at first contemplated on behalf of purely commercial interests.   The troubles which occurred in East Africa
towards the close of 1888 led to the employment there of both
naval and military forces, an eventuality which the Radicals in
the Reichstag professed to have foreseen.   When the intervention

of the Empire was debated in January, 1889, the Chancellor used words which showed that his heart was not thoroughly won to the colony movement. "To this day," he said, "I am not a 'colony man,' and I entertain the gravest apprehensions on the subject, but I was compelled to yield to the general demand of the nation. I ask the assent of the lawful Assembly of the Empire to my action. If it repudiates my action, I can only admit that I have been mistaken. I shall then give up all further plans. The coast territory had been acquired by a German company. It is, at all events, very important and must be retained. I cannot burden myself with the reproach of posterity that I failed to protect Germans and German possessions. Neither in three weeks, nor three months, no, nor in three years, can one look for results ; but perhaps in thirty years' time people may bitterly rue the neglect of to-day. If the locomotive of the Empire has struck out a track for itself, I will not be the one to throw stones in its way." It is not to be denied, too, that the national enthusiasm for colonial enterprise has somewhat cooled down after it has been found by experience that the way to foreign empire lies through sacrifice both of life and treasure.[1]

---

[1] Naturally enough the colonial movement has called into existence a host of societies, associations, and companies, including (1) the German East African Company ; (2) German Colonial Association ; (3) Society for German Colonisation ; (4) New Guinea Company ; (5) East African Plantation Company ; (6) Colonial Society for South-West Africa ; (7) Vitu Company ; (8) German West African Company ; (9) Central Association for Commercial Geography and the Promotion of German Interests Abroad ; (10) West German Association for Colonisation and Export ; (11) South Brazil Colonisation Society ; (12) German Society for South America ; and (13) Hermann Society for German Colonisation in South America.

Since the above chapter was written, a Colonial Department has been formed at the German Foreign Office under Dr. Krauel.

APPENDIX.

A.—WAGNER'S STATE SOCIALISTIC PROGRAMME.

(*See Chapter I., page* 12.)

In the first of two articles—important for the studying of his position—contributed in 1887 to the *Tübinger Zeitschrift,* Professor Wagner formulates a systematic State Socialistic programme as follows :—

" I. A better system of production, by means of which production may above all things be assured an ordered course, instead of the utterly irregular one which prevails at present. Prevention of the employment of 'economic conjunctures' by individuals at the expense of others ; therefore, checks against speculation. More comprehensive participation by the mass of the population, especially by the working classes, but also by other people in humble positions, in the material benefits and the blessings of civilisation caused by the increase of the productive forces ; therefore, increase of wages both absolutely and relatively, considered as a quota of the produce, assured employment, restriction of the hours of labour, especially of daily labour, to an extent called for by sanitary and moral considerations, and suited to technical circumstances at any given time, the term varying, of course, in different branches of production ; exclusion, as far as possible, of children from paid employments, especially when the conditions are sanitarily and morally dangerous ; similar restriction of female work, particularly in factories ; adequate precautions against accidents during employment and provision for their consequences ; insurance against sickness, incapacity, and old age, with provision for widows and orphans. Consequently special development of all the legal maxims, both in public and civil law, measures, and institutions which are included in the catchwords 'protection of the working-man' and 'industrial insurance,' or 'industrial insurance legislation.'

" II. Inclusion in the administrative duties of the State, the parish, and the other public bodies of such measures as conduce to the moral, intellectual, sanitary, physical, economic, and social advancement of the mass of the people ; so far as may seem necessary and expedient the expenditure of public money for these purposes, without fear of the 'public Communism' which would to some extent be thereby encouraged. This implies the recognition of the principle of State help—legislative, administrative, and financial—for the lower classes conjointly with self-help and the co-operative system.

"III. Adjustment of financial arrangements in such manner that a larger part of the national income, which now falls, in the form of rent, interest, undertaker's profits, and profits from 'conjunctures' [profits due to speculation, chance, spontaneous increase in values, etc.], to the class possessing land and capital and carrying on private undertakings, may be diverted into public channels. Transference to the State, parish, etc., of such land, capital, and undertakings as may economically and technically be well managed in public hands, and such as most easily develop in private hands into actual monopolies, peculiarly tend to enterprise on a great scale, or even now are carried on by public companies, a form of undertakership which in its advantages and defects approximates to public enterprise both economically and technically. . . . (Here Wagner proposes to place such undertakings and institutions as means of communication and transport, the banking and insurance systems, water and gas works, markets, etc., in the hands of the State or the parish. His idea is that the State and public bodies would and should deal more considerately and generously with their officials and employees generally than private undertakers and capitalists, and that their good example would be a social blessing.)

"IV. Public revenue to be so raised as to allow of the 'Communistic' character of public bodies, above described, being developed wherever decided objections, consequent upon the peculiar circumstances of the case, do not exist. This 'Communistic' character to be strengthened in favour of the poorer and socially weaker classes, with whom the economic and social struggle for existence and for social advancement is severest, by means of a system of administrative measures calculated especially to benefit them, yet the cost of which shall be defrayed by the general revenue and taxes. But this 'Communistic' character of State activity to be weaker where the interests of the well-to-do and richer classes of society come especially or exclusively into question. Here expenditure should be rather covered by a just system of taxes—including taxes based on the principle of taxation according to benefit—than by the use of the general revenue. This implies the regulation of the post, telegraph, and railway tariffs, judicial charges, school fees, etc.

" V. Taxation to be so adjusted that, besides fulfilling its primary function, that of providing the revenue needed to cover public requirements, it may as well as possible fulfil a not less important indirect purpose, which is twofold : (1) regulative interference with the distribution of the income and wealth of private persons, so far as that distribution is the product of free economic intercourse—as by the medium of prices, wages, interest, and rent—with a view to counteracting the harshness, injustice, and excessive privileges caused by the distribution obtaining in this intercourse ; (2) and at the same time regulative interference, supported necessarily by further administrative measures, and eventually by compulsion (as in the domain of industrial insurance) in private consumption. This latter can be done by making the lower classes provide—by means of direct and indirect taxes, especially indirect (excise), which in this connection are often very suitable—the revenue necessary for administrative purposes calculated to benefit them, this being effected by diverting income which they may be applying to improper, perhaps injurious, or at least less necessary and wholesome purposes (*e.g.*, drink), to purposes more beneficial to society, the class, or the individual. This two-sided policy of taxation I call social. The second side here advanced . . . is based, as concerns the mass of the population, the lower labouring classes, on the assumption that in the truest interests of the nation a guardianship may and must be exercised over the national consumption or over the application of income to personal purposes."

B.—THE " BUBBLE PERIOD" OF 1873.

(*See Chapter IV., page* 40.)

Some official statistics employed by the Government in justifying a new Company Law introduced in the Reichstag and passed June 28th, 1884, throw vivid light upon the financial rogueries of this period. It appears that there had liquidated up to that year—

Of 203	companies established	before	1871,	30, or 15		per cent.		
,, 203	,,	,,	in	1871,	52	,, 25·6	,,	,,
,, 478	,,	,,	,,	1872,	138	,, 29	,,	,,
,, 162	,,	,,	,,	1873,	67	,, 41	,,	,,
,, 30	,,	,,	,,	1874,	14	,, 47	,,	,,
,, 3	,,	,,	,,	1875,	none			
,, 25	,,	,,	after	1875,	3, or 12		,,	,,
,, 63	,,	,,	time unknown,	14, ,, 22·2			,,	,,

Further, there had gone into bankruptcy—

When established.		Percentage.				Marks.
Before 1871	11	5·4	with paid-up capital of			49,829,124
In 1871	14	6·9	,,	,,	,, ,,	16,484,337
,, 1872	37	7·9	,,	,,	,, ,,	59,404,530
,, 1873	8	5·6	,,	,,	,, ,,	4,995,000
,, 1874	5	16·7	,,	,,	,, ,,	1,625,000
,, 1875	1	33·3	,,	,,	,, ,,	2,550,000
After 1875	1	4	,,	,,	,, ,,	1,800,000
Time unknown	2	—	,,	,,	,, ,,	960,000
						137,647,991

The net result was that of the 203 companies founded in 1871, 35 reduced their capital, 52 liquidated, and 14 went into bankruptcy ; of the 478 companies founded in 1872, 91 reduced their capital, 138 liquidated, and 38 went into bankruptcy ; and of the 168 companies which fell to 1873, 22 reduced their capital, 67 liquidated, and 9 went into bankruptcy. The loss to shareholders could not be accurately fixed, but by liquidations and bankruptcies a loss of 345,628,054 marks had been suffered up to 1884.

C.—THE TOBACCO MONOPOLY BILL.

(*See Chapter VI., page* 67.)

A momentous project of State Socialism such as is contained in the Tobacco Monopoly Bill deserves nearer examination. The measure which the Reichstag was asked to adopt in 1882 provided that the manufacture of raw tobacco and the production of manufactured tobacco should only take place in establishments appointed for the purpose by the *régie*, except in so far as tobacco leaves required manipulation at the hands of the planters and the authorised dealers in raw tobacco. The re-manufacture of products supplied by the *régie*, and the manufacture out of other materials than tobacco of products intended to take the place of smoking tobacco, snuff, or " twist," were prohibited. Manufactures of tobacco could only be sold within the territory of the monopoly by persons authorised by the *régie*. It was proposed to establish an Imperial Tobacco Office, the head of which should be the Imperial Chancellor. This authority should have the supreme administration of the monopoly, but certain powers were to be devolved upon the various Governments, which should appoint the vendors of tobacco. The customs and excise department would be responsible for the control of tobacco-cultivation, the sanction and control of trade in tobacco; the control of imports, exports, and transit of raw and manufactured tobacco, as well as the watching of the frontiers for the prevention of illicit traffic. As to the cultivation of tobacco in Germany, it was proposed to allot each year's requirements amongst the various States, according to a proportion to be always fixed by the average area cultivated during the six preceding years. The Governments of the States would, however, determine in which excise districts and parishes the cultivation of tobacco should be carried on for the *régie* and for export.

For the production of manufactured tobacco for the *régie*, it was proposed to establish raw tobacco warehouses and tobacco manufactories, but the preparation of tobacco might still be carried on as a house industry under control of the authorities. The existing location of the tobacco industry in the various States was to be made the standard for the continuance and extension of the same. Tobacco manufactories were to be exempted from taxation either by State or parish. It was also provided that the raw tobacco required by the *régie* should to the minimum extent of two-fifths be of home production. Other provisions related to prices and the introduction of foreign tobacco by travellers. The bill provided for the compensation of all persons who should suffer by the prohibition of the private manufacture and sale of tobacco products. Manufacturers and dealers in raw tobacco whose factories or warehouses were depreciated by reason of the introduction of the monopoly would receive money compensation equal to the decrease in value unless the buildings were acquired by the *régie*. Tobacco manufacturers not selling their factories to the *régie* and dealers in raw tobacco would also receive compensation proportionate to the diminution of their earnings, provided that they had been engaged in the tobacco trade for at least four years, dating from the publication of the law, and that their business was a source of livelihood. Personal compensation of this kind would be based on the average net profits of a business during the years 1876 to 1881, but with the exclusion of the best and the worst business year, and would be as follows :—

Duration of business.	Manufacturers.	Dealers in raw tobacco.
4 to 5 years exclus.	2 times	1 { times the average yearly net profits.
5 ,, 6 ,,	$2\frac{1}{2}$,,	$1\frac{1}{6}$,, ,, ,,
6 ,, 7 ,,	3 ,,	$1\frac{2}{6}$,, ,, ,,
7 ,, 8 ,,	$3\frac{1}{2}$,,	$1\frac{3}{6}$,, ,, ,,
8 ,, 9 ,,	4 ,,	$1\frac{4}{6}$,, ,, ,,
9 ,, 10 ,,	$4\frac{1}{2}$,,	$1\frac{5}{6}$,, ,, ,,
10 years and over	5 ,,	2 ,, ,, ,,

By net profits was to be understood the gross revenue after deduction of business costs and 5 per cent. interest on invested capital. Compensation was also to be allowed to all dealers in tobacco products and all adult workpeople in the tobacco industry and trade who were not retained in the service of the *régie*. The same principle being followed as in the compensation of manufacturers and raw tobacco dealers, the indemnities payable were as follows:—

Duration of employment.	Workpeople employed in the manufacture of tobacco.	Tobacco dealers and employers in the tobacco trade.
4 to 5 years exclus.	2 times	1 { times the average yearly salary, wages, or net profits.
5 ,, 6 ,,	$2\frac{1}{2}$,,	$1\frac{1}{6}$,, ,, ,,
6 ,, 7 ,,	3 ,,	$1\frac{2}{6}$,, ,, ,,
7 ,, 8 ,,	$3\frac{1}{2}$,,	$1\frac{3}{6}$,, ,, ,,
8 ,, 9 ,,	4 ,,	$1\frac{4}{6}$,, ,, ,,
9 ,, 10 ,,	$4\frac{1}{2}$,,	$1\frac{5}{6}$,, ,, ,,
10 years and over	5 ,,	2 ,, ,, ,,

The concluding provisions laid down conditions for the cultivation, sale, and export of tobacco, specified the control to be exercised by the authorities, and fixed the penalties incurred by reason of infringement of the law. The net revenue from the monopoly was to be handed over to the States in the measure of their share in the population of the monopoly area. It was proposed that the law should enter into force on January 1st, 1883, so far as regarded the cultivation of tobacco, and the rest of the provisions on July 1st following, except that trade with tobacco products would be allowed as before until January 1st, 1884.

The Government drew out a balance sheet for the first year of the monopoly as follows:—

RECEIPTS.

Sale of 1,512,998 cwts. of products:

			Marks.
587,528 cwts. of cigars	. . . . .	.	280,413,947
749,857 ,,	smoking tobacco	. . .	67,187,169
122,425 ,,	snuff	. . .	15,548,051
45,910 ,,	" twist " tobacco	. . .	8,378,502
2,628 ,,	cigarettes . .	. . .	1,011,780
4,650 ,,	foreign cigars .	. . .	16,030,875
			388,570,324
Deduct sale fees	. . . . .	.	40,799,882
Gross revenue of the *régie* .	. . .	.	347,770,442

EXPENDITURE.

		Marks.
1. General management.	.	385,000
2. Management of manufactories and warehouses .	.	2,314,000
3. Wages:		
(a) 81,000 workpeople at 577 Mks. . .	.	46,737,000
(b) 1,000 overseers at 1,200 ,, . .	.	1,200,000
4. Cost of raw material :		
(a) Foreign tobacco { 93,912 cwts. at 144 Mks.	.	13,523,328
{ 845,214 ,, 55·80 ,,	.	47,162,942
(b) Home tobacco, 626,084 cwts. at 35 Mks.	.	21,912,940

Marks.

5. Purchase of 4,650 cwts. of foreign cigars=32,550
     thousand at 200 Mks. per 1000   6,510,000
6. Materials, etc. 16,379,565
7. Supervision of tobacco cultivation 1,000,000
8. Transport of raw tobacco and finished products . 5,500,000
9. Maintenance of buildings and repairs of machinery . 1,200,000
10. Interest on a capital (including the reserve) of
      220,000,000 Mks., and redemption of the same, to-
      gether 4¼ per cent.   9,350,000
                                                   ——————— 173,174,775

                            Leaving a balance of .   . 174,595,667
Deduct further the interest on the aggregate amount of compensation, estimated at 257,000,000 Mks., at 4¼ per cent., including redemption   10,922,500
                                                   ———————
                     Net revenue   .   .   . 163,673,167

                         or something over £8,000,000

D.—RESOLUTIONS OF THE LABOUR CONFERENCE.

(*See Chapter VIII., page* 108.)

The International Labour Conference, which met in Berlin on
March 15th, 1890, sat for exactly a fortnight. The resolutions adopted
regarding the questions submitted are as follows :—

I. REGULATION OF WORK IN MINES.

(A) *Should underground employment be prohibited in the case* (1) *of children
under a certain age, and* (2) *in the case of females ?*

It is desirable (1) that the lowest limit of age at which children
should be admitted to underground work in mines be gradually
and as much as possible raised to the age of 14, while for southern
countries this limit might be fixed at 12 years ; (2) that underground
work should be forbidden for females.

(B) *Should a restriction of the duration of the shifts be prescribed for mines in
which work is particularly dangerous to health ?*

It is desirable that, in cases where engineering skill has not succeeded in obviating the dangers to health which are a natural risk,
or are incidental to the peculiar manner of working certain mines, the
duration of the shifts should be limited, the putting in practice of this
suggestion, either by law or administrative measure, or by agreement
between employer and workmen, or otherwise, being left to each
country, according to its principles and practice.

(C) *Is it possible to subject work in mines to international regulations in order to
assure regularity in the output of coal ?*

It is desirable that the engineers entrusted with the working of the
mines should, without exception, be men whose experience and capa-

bilities have been duly tested. That the relations between the miners and the mining engineers should, as far as possible, be direct, and thus calculated to foster a feeling of mutual confidence and respect. That a continuous effort should be made to increase the measures of prevention and relief which each country, according to its customs, has organised to protect the workman and his family against the consequences of illness, misfortune, premature incapacitation, old age, or death, and which are designed to improve the lot of the miner and to attach him to his calling. That an effort should be made in order to ensure continuity in the production of coal to obviate strikes. Experience shows that the best means of preventing strikes is for masters and men, in all cases where their differences cannot be adjusted by direct agreement, to agree to invoke the decision of an arbiter.

II. REGULATION OF SUNDAY LABOUR.

(A) *Should work as a rule be prohibited on Sunday except in case of need?*

It is desirable (1) that without prejudice to the exceptions necessary in each country, or to the requisite postponements of the day, one day of rest in each week should be ensured to all protected persons (children, youths, and women) ; (2) that one day of rest should be allowed to all industrial workmen ; (3) that the day of rest for protected workmen should fall on the Sunday ; and (4) that the day of rest for industrial workmen should also fall on a Sunday.

(B) *What exceptions should be allowed?*

Exceptions are permissible (1) with regard to occupations which on technical grounds necessitate continuity of production, or which supply to the public necessary products whereof delivery must be made daily ; (2) with regard to certain occupations which on account of their nature can only be pursued at certain seasons of the year, or which are dependent on the irregular working of natural forces. Even in the case of such exceptions, the workmen should have every other Sunday free.

(C) *Should these exceptions be determined by international agreement, by law, or by administrative measures?*

With a view to determining the exceptions on uniform principles, it is desirable that their definite regulation should be by arrangement between the various Governments.

III. Regulation of Children's Labour.

(A) *Should children up to a certain age be excluded from industrial work?*

It is desirable that children of both sexes who have not yet reached a certain age should be prohibited from being employed in industrial occupations.

(B) *How is the age to which such a prohibition shall continue to be fixed, and should the age be the same or different in various branches of industry?*

It is desirable that the limit should be fixed at 12 years, save in southern countries, where it might be 10 years, and that the limit of age should be the same for all industrial occupations without exception.

(C) *What restrictions should be imposed on the time and manner of employment for children within the permissible limit?*

It is desirable that the children should previously have fulfilled the requirements of elementary education ; that children under 14 should not work either at night or on Sunday ; that the aggregate hours of work should not amount to more than six hours, with an interval of at least half an hour ; that children should be prohibited from engaging in unhealthy or dangerous occupations, or at least should only be permitted to do so under protective conditions.

IV. Regulation of Youths' Labour.

(A) *Should the industrial work of young persons who have passed the age of childhood be restricted, and, if so, up to what age?*

It is desirable that young workpeople of both sexes between 14 and 16 should neither work at night nor on Sundays.

(B) *What restriction should be prescribed?*

It is desirable that the aggregate daily hours of work should not exceed ten, with intervals amounting in all to at least one hour and a half.

(C) *Are deviations from the general rule to be allowed for certain branches of industry?*

It is desirable that for particular branches of industry certain exceptions should be allowed ; that for unhealthy and dangerous occupations restrictions should be imposed ; and that young people between 16 and 18 should be assured a certain measure of protection as far as regards (1) maximum day's work, (2) night work, (3) Sunday labour, and (4) employment in peculiarly unhealthy and dangerous occupations.

V. Regulation of Female Labour.

Should the work of married women be restricted by day or by night? Should the work of all females (women and girls) be subjected to certain restrictions? What restrictions would be advisable? Should exceptions be provided for in the case of individual branches of industry, and, if so, for which?

It is desirable (1) that girls and women above 16 years of age should not work either at night or on Sundays. (2) That the total number of working hours should not exceed eleven daily, and with intervals amounting, in all, to at least one hour and a half. (3) That exceptions should be admissible for certain branches of industry. (4) That restrictions should be imposed in the case of occupations especially unhealthy and dangerous. (5) That mothers should only be allowed to return to work four weeks after their confinement.

E.—PRINCE BISMARCK'S VIEWS ON EMIGRATION.

(*See Chapter XI., page* 147.)

Prince Bismarck's views on emigration are so interesting that it is well worth while to quote several passages from his speeches bearing upon the subject. Speaking in the Reichstag on June 14th, 1882, he said :—

" I have often drawn attention to the fact that emigration is not a consequence of over-population, for the emigration is smallest from the over-populated parts of the country ; it is greatest from the least populous provinces. . . . Why do people emigrate especially from the agricultural provinces? Because these parts have no industry, and because the industry which was formerly tolerably busy there has been overburdened and suffocated by free trade. Frederick the Great fostered industry in those provinces. Every small town in Pomerania, Posen, and West Prussia had a large woollen and cloth industry, and isolated remains still exist ; there are also woollen weaving works, but they are in decay. After the provinces of Pomerania, Posen, and West Prussia [in extent of emigration] come Mecklenburg and Schleswig-Holstein. Hanover is also largely represented, because, apart from a few centres, particularly the city of Hanover, it has little industry. In a purely agricultural population the career which a labourer can follow is straightforward and without change ; when he is twenty-eight or thirty years old he is able to overlook it to the end ; he knows how much he can earn, and he knows that it is impossible by means of an agricultural occupation to raise himself above his condition. . . .

In industry a workman cannot foresee how his life will close, even if he should not raise himself above the common level, and should have no connections. We have very many manufacturers who, in one or two generations, have risen from being simple artisans into millionaires, powerful and important men ; I need not name any such men to you—the names are on everybody's lips, and they are also on the lips of the working-man. For the artisan industry has the marshal's *baton*, which it is said the French soldier carries in his knapsack : this raises and animates the hope of the artisan, and he does not need to become a millionaire. Industry furnishes a thousand examples—such as I have myself seen in the province of Pomerania, little affected though it is by industry—of how the man who as agricultural labourer never gets beyond ordinary day wages, can in the factory, as soon as he shows more skill than others, earn much higher wages, and eventually rise to the position of overseer, and even higher ; indeed, skilled workmen, who often go farther as self-taught men than the most learned technologists, may hope to become partners of their employers. The prospect keeps the hope active, and at the same time increases the pleasure in work. Industry and agriculture should supplement each other ; industry is the consumer of the local agrarian products which agriculture could not otherwise sell in a waste district, and on the other hand, the farmer is the customer of industry, in case he has money. I believe that the lack of an industry—in other words, the lack of protection for national labour and of protective duties—is, equally with the pressure of direct taxation, the great cause why the least populous provinces have the greatest emigration. It is the destruction of hope in a man that drives him to emigration. The *terra incognita* abroad offers him every prospect of being something *there*, though it has been impossible *here*. This is why rural labourers emigrate—because they have no industry in their neighbourhood, and because they cannot in retail convert the produce of their labour into money." Prince Bismarck advanced the same theories, though in less detail, in the Reichstag on March 8th, 1879.

Again, he said, on June 26th, 1884 :—

"I combat the promotion of emigration. A German who puts away his fatherland as he would an old coat is no longer a German for me ; I no longer regard him as a fellow-subject."

On January 8th, 1885, he said :—

"There are two kinds of emigrants : first, those who emigrate because they still possess the needful money ; and then those whom I would call the mal-contents." At the same time he added : "The statistics of emigration are a thoroughly accurate measure of the increase of our prosperity. The better off we are, the greater the emigration. The fact that the emigration of 1880-81 was higher than before is a proof that protective duties have had an effect upon our industry, and that there were many more people in that year who possessed money necessary for the sea passage and the purchase of land. That alone is the index of emigration. In the years of atrophy, when we had free trade, emigration decreased because people had not money enough to pay for their sea passage and for land. In the year 1871-72, when everybody with us felt himself rich, owing to the French milliards, there were again more people ready to emigrate. I allow that under certain circumstances the desire to escape military service, and, with peasantry, the desire to escape land taxes and high parochial taxes, may also exert an influence, but, on the whole, increasing emigration is an irrefutable proof of increasing wealth and earnings." He spoke, of course, for Germany, and explained that in Ireland it was different, adding that there the people had "less emigrated than been emigrated" at the cost of others.

INDEX.